ERNESTO 'CHE' GUEVARA was born in Argentina in 1928. He trained as a doctor and travelled extensively around Latin America. He played a key role, alongside Fidel Castro, in the revolution in Cuba and, after the three-year guerrilla war, became Minister for Industry. He also established a guerrilla base in Bolivia. He was captured and killed in 1967.

By the same author

The Motorcycle Diaries
Reminiscences of the Cuban Revolutionary War
The Bolivian Diary

ERNESTO 'CHE' GUEVARA

Guerrilla Warfare

THE AUTHORISED EDITION
WITH CORRECTIONS MADE BY
ERNESTO 'CHE' GUEVARA

Foreword by Harry 'Pombo' Villegas

HARPER PERENNIAL

London, New York, Toronto, Sydney and New Delhi

Harper Perennial
An imprint of HarperCollins*Publishers*
77–85 Fulham Palace Road
Hammersmith
London W6 8JB

www.harperperennial.co.uk
Visit our authors' blog at www.fifthestate.co.uk

This Harper Perennial edition published 2009
1

This version of the text first published by Ocean Press in 2006

Published in Spanish as *La Guerra de Guerrillas*

A catalogue record for this book
is available from the British Library

ISBN 978-0-00-727720-9

Printed and bound in Great Britain by Clays Ltd, St Ives plc

Mixed Sources
Product group from well-managed
forests and other controlled sources
www.fsc.org Cert no. SW-COC-1806
© 1996 Forest Stewardship Council

FSC

FSC is a non-profit international organisation established to promote the
responsible management of the world's forests. Products carrying the FSC
label are independently certified to assure consumers that they come
from forests that are managed to meet the social, economic and
ecological needs of present and future generations.

Find out more about HarperCollins and the environment at
www.harpercollins.co.uk/green

CONTENTS

Chapter III
Organization of the Guerrilla Front

Chapter IV
Appendices

EDITORIAL NOTE

For many readers around the world, the publication of the essential writings of historic figures has a high symbolic value, given that they represent a perspective on a particular era and, in turn, a form of living memory of the author themselves.

This is one of the aims behind this publication of *Guerrilla Warfare*, which was written by Che Guevara between 1960 and 1961, and published immediately. The book, however, has its own history and evolution that, we venture to say, has surpassed the expectations of its author, who by preparing a manual on guerrilla warfare intended to systematize rules, to theorize a practical experience (the guerrilla struggle in Cuba), define its structures, and draw out some generalizations.

Due to this book's form, content, and Che's sharp and concise style, it very soon found an echo in the revolutionary movements of the 1960s, reflected in Che's description of the new type of guerrilla fighter and the essential role that they should play as a social reformer and catalyst for full social justice.

This clearly explains why the manual very soon also became a widely studied text in US counterinsurgency schools and military academies.

The course of historical events led Che to embark on a new front in the struggle in the Congo in 1965, his memories of which are recorded in *Reminiscences of the Revolutionary War: Congo*. This experience, despite the importance of its objectives, did not produce the expected results; a retreat was forced upon Che and the Cuban combatants who had been mobilized to support the struggle following a request made by the Organization of African Unity. It was decided that Che would leave the Congo, first to travel to Tanzania and later to Prague, the place chosen for the preparation of future battles. He remained in Prague until July 1966, when he returned incognito to Cuba to begin the military training that would lead him to Bolivia.

During his time in Prague, among the tasks Che assumed was a revision of *Guerrilla Warfare*, based on a suggestion made by Fidel Castro in a letter dated June 3, 1966.

Fidel wrote:

> I read the entire draft of the book about your experience in the C.* and reread the manual on guerrilla warfare, so as to be able to make the best possible analysis... Although in an immediate sense, there is no point in talking to you about these issues, for the time being I will limit myself to telling you that I found the work on the C. extremely interesting and I think that the effort you made to leave a written account of everything was really worthwhile. In relation to the manual on guerrilla warfare, it seems to me that it should be updated a bit in view of the new experiences accumulated in the field, to introduce some new ideas and to emphasize certain questions that are absolutely fundamental.

Che had very little time for revising the text between receiving the letter from Fidel and the date of his return to Cuba, which explains the mechanisms used for the changes that were introduced, especially in terms of his suggestions for a future and more complete expansion of the text. The method used

---

*   Fidel is referring to the Congo, Africa.

maintained the style that Che always employed — the use of several colors (red, blue, and green) — as well as annotations in the margin pointing to the need to consult, consider, and expand on different points. Many of the notes remained on the level of mere observations that could not be developed for obvious reasons. At the same time, the comprehensive and temporal vision of Che's new observations is displayed, for example, when he writes, "correct this in accordance with the Vietnamese [experience]."

Given the testimonial and historical value of the annotations made by Che, the present edition of *Guerrilla Warfare* incorporates them with their corresponding explanations and places them in boldface in the text and footnotes, so as to make them more intelligible to the reader.

The Che Guevara Studies Center and Ocean Press, as part of their joint publishing project, and particularly in relation to Che's classic texts, wish to offer the reader the definitive, albeit unfinished version of a work that is always present and permanently being renewed, as Che suggested in the first edition in his dedication to Camilo: "This work is dedicated to Camilo Cienfuegos, who should have read and corrected it, but whose fate prevented him from carrying out the task."

The editors

ERNESTO CHE GUEVARA

One of *Time* magazine's "icons of the century," Ernesto Guevara de la Serna was born in Rosario, Argentina, on June 14, 1928. He made several trips around Latin America during and immediately after his studies at medical school in Buenos Aires, including his 1952 journey with Alberto Granado, on the unreliable Norton motorbike described in his travel journal *The Motorcycle Diaries*.

He was already becoming involved in political activity and living in Guatemala when, in 1954, the elected government of Jacobo Árbenz was overthrown in a CIA-organized military operation. Ernesto escaped to Mexico, profoundly radicalized.

Following up on a contact made in Guatemala, Guevara sought out the group of exiled Cuban revolutionaries in Mexico City. In July 1955, he met Fidel Castro and immediately enlisted in the guerrilla expedition to overthrow the Cuban dictator Fulgencio Batista. The Cubans nicknamed him "Che," a popular form of address in Argentina.

On November 25, 1956, Che Guevara set sail for Cuba aboard the yacht *Granma* as the doctor to the guerrilla group that began the revolutionary armed struggle in Cuba's Sierra Maestra mountains. Within several months, he was named by Fidel Castro as the first Rebel Army commander, though he continued ministering medically to wounded guerrilla fighters and captured soldiers from Batista's army.

In September 1958, Che Guevara played a decisive role in the military defeat of Batista after he and Camilo Cienfuegos led separate guerrilla columns westward from the Sierra Maestra (later described in his book *Reminiscences of the Cuban Revolutionary War*).

After Batista fled on January 1, 1959, Che Guevara became a key leader of the new revolutionary government, first as head of the Industrial Department of the National Institute of Agrarian Reform, then as president of the National Bank. In February 1961 he became minister of industry. He was also a central leader of the political organization that in 1965 became the Communist Party of Cuba.

Apart from these responsibilities, Che Guevara often represented the Cuban revolutionary government around the world, heading numerous delegations and speaking at the United Nations and other international forums in Asia, Africa, Latin America, and the socialist bloc countries. He earned a reputation as a passionate and articulate spokesperson for Third World peoples, most famously at the 1961 conference at Punta del Este in Uruguay, where he denounced US President Kennedy's Alliance for Progress.

As had been his intention since joining the Cuban revolutionary movement, Che Guevara left Cuba in April 1965, initially to lead a Cuban-organized guerrilla mission to support the revolutionary struggle in the Congo. He returned to Cuba secretly in December 1965, to prepare another Cuban-organized guerrilla force for Bolivia. Arriving in Bolivia in November 1966, Che's plan was to challenge that country's military dictatorship and eventually to instigate a revolutionary movement that would extend throughout the continent of Latin America. He was wounded and captured by US-trained and run Bolivian counterinsurgency troops on October 8, 1967. The following day he was murdered and his body hidden.

Che Guevara's remains were finally discovered in 1997 and returned to Cuba. A memorial was built at Santa Clara in central Cuba, where he had won a major military battle during the revolutionary war.

FOREWORD

The request of the Che Guevara Studies Center to prepare a few brief notes for a foreword to the new edition of Che's *Guerrilla Warfare*, which he later updated during his stay in Prague after the end of his campaign in the Congo, represents for me an immense commitment.

Che's theoretical creativity, characterized by his multi-disciplinary approach and backed by his coherent practice in relation to his ideas, offers for progressive people throughout the world — and especially the young — unquestionable guiding values. This is why the desire expressed in the Cuban Pioneers' slogan to "be like Che" continues to be valid for almost all of humanity in its quest for full social justice.

Demonstrating the versatile nature of Che's creative activity, *Guerrilla Warfare* brings together the theoretical-practical experience of the revolutionary war in Cuba, synthesizing the strategy and tactics of the Cuban revolution during the struggle for power. The book also brings together the military thinking behind that process in the insurrectional stage, and the military activities of Fidel Castro as its leader, and its vanguard of Raúl Castro, Juan Almeida, Camilo Cienfuegos, and Che Guevara. It was Che who assumed responsibility for objectively analyzing and generalizing this experience, with the aim of providing the necessary theoretical framework that is indispensable for those who in the future might adopt this method of struggle.

For many analysts of revolutionary war in different parts of the world, *Guerrilla Warfare* is one of the texts that discusses the topic most systematically.

Since its first publication, these qualities have not escaped the attention of US military analysts, who have incorporated it as a text to be studied and used in the preparation of counter-insurgency forces (such as the Green Berets). These forces were created and trained as a military response to the upsurge in revolutionary movements — and especially the guerrilla struggles that were developing in Latin America — following the victory of the Cuban revolution.

As is obvious, the validity of the ideas contained in this book was recognized by the empire's think tanks when they were analyzing the causes that generated this phenomenon in Cuba. They have also studied the strategic alternatives proposed by the leaders of the Cuban revolution in relation to changes that should be incorporated in light of new experiences of social transformation.

The imperialist enemy has tried to respond and offer possible ways to combat these ideas. One such initiative was the so-called Alliance for Progress, which was established in 1961 with the objective of preventing a repetition of the Cuban revolution elsewhere in the region, arguing that it was an isolated or exceptional case. The objectives established after the victory of the revolution in 1959 are still being pursued today with new treaties such as the Free Trade Area of the Americas (FTAA), which has the identical goals of subjugation and exploitation.

This explains why Che felt compelled to analyze the Cuban experience in light of revolutionary theory and practice in a way that could be applied to other peoples' struggles. From this arose the need for *Guerrilla Warfare* to offer a methodology, a guide, and a way to take political power in Latin America through the means of armed struggle.

The starting point for the ideas underlying this manual are the conditions of exploitation prevailing in the region and their social consequences, conditions which generate illiteracy and inadequate health care, unemployment, and overwhelming impoverishment in almost all the countries of the hemisphere. This is the result of the domination imposed by governing oligarchies that are the unconditional allies of the United States, and that are responsible for obstructing the appropriate roads to resolving these scourges, thereby impeding a more just society.

Given the weight of such negative and harmful conditions, it was clear that there was no other alternative but to resort to violence in response to the intimidation that was imposed. Therefore, for Che, employing the guerrilla struggle was the most appropriate and certain road, although it was also the one that required the most sacrifice.

It should also be considered that the response conceptualized by Che was not only the concrete result of a revolutionary theory and practice, but was also an attempt to incorporate and apply a specific methodology and didactic approach to this form of struggle. Che seeks to clearly define the advantages of the method to be utilized to achieve success, in what are known as the "seven golden rules" of the guerrilla struggle, as well as to define the risks and dangers that might lead to failure.

Military thinking, in its theoretical dimension, is defined in revolutionary terms as the range of concepts, ideas, and principles held by an individual or group regarding the way to conduct war. In general, these experiences are imparted in writing, as in Che's classic works such as *Reminiscences of the Cuban Revolutionary War* and *Reminiscences of the Revolutionary War: Congo*, "Guerrilla Warfare: A Method," and this book, *Guerrilla Warfare*.

Other methods are transmitted based on the experiences derived from practical activities, battles, military operations, and the conduct of war. In the concrete case of Cuba, the main example and maximum exponent of this is Fidel.

Many will ask, 45 years after *Guerrilla Warfare* was first published, whether the ideas proposed by Che retain their validity as the way to take political power under current conditions. To respond requires returning to the main lines of Che's thought; as a Marxist, he offered an objective analysis and a coherent approach in dealing with reality in time, form, and space, which was indispensable for the analysis and elaboration of his political-military theses.

The possibility of applying these theses and achieving success in irregular warfare through the guerrilla struggle was based on the limited possibility of finding other ways to realize the dreams and ideals of the masses. For Che, the role of the guerrilla fighter was to be a catalyst that could accelerate the conditions of struggle among the people, consistent with the principle that the role of the revolutionary is not to sit back and wait to see the cadaver of imperialism pass by, but to facilitate the conditions that lead to its collapse.

For Cubans, the need for revolutionary war and its combative spirit remains valid as the only way to defend ourselves against our potential enemy, Yankee imperialism, and to preserve the revolution and the social justice we have achieved. This is implicit in our military doctrine of the War of All the People, a strategy designed to provide each citizen with a way of participating in the fight, by which guerrilla warfare continues to be a genuine mass struggle.

For Che, the people are to the guerrilla fighters what water is to a fish, that is, their means of existence. On the tactical level, the "seven golden rules" remain valid, in so far as if creatively applied they would guarantee victory:

- Do not engage in a fight that cannot be won.
- Move continuously, hit and run.
- Use the enemy as the main supplier of weapons.
- Hide your movements.
- Make use of the element of surprise in military actions.
- Form new columns once some power has been won.
- In general, proceed through three phases: strategic defense, balance between the possibilities of enemy action and guerrilla action, and finally the total annihilation of the adversary.

In short, all this is conducted using the tactics of the guerrilla: mobility, nocturnal movement, flexibility, ability to surprise, rapidity of attack, the care and rationing of supplies, and rapid alternation between concentrating efforts and decentralizing.

At the present time, as a result of the disintegration of the socialist camp, the dislocation of most of the forces of the left, and the consolidation of a hegemonic world order, the enemy has been forced, in the specific case of Latin America, to introduce superficial changes in its methods of oppression and colonial domination. Military dictatorships have been replaced by pseudo-democratic governments, subordinate, as always, to imperialism's dictates and orders, making false promises to try to solve the serious problems that our people suffer as a result of neoliberalism and the consequences of underdevelopment

— problems that the oligarchies and the transnationals have never been interested in solving.

In the case of progressive governments that have gained office through the electoral road, taking advantage of the so-called democratic opening, they have projected social programs with the aim of improving their peoples' situation. The immediate reaction of the imperialists has been to accuse them of being terrorists, of forming part of the "axis of evil," and so on. This has been accompanied by different types and methods of aggression employed with the intention of blocking plans that would benefit the popular sectors. Logically, this leads to confrontation, and does not exclude the possibility that under specific conditions, after exhausting the democratic road, it will be necessary to resort to violence and return to the fundamental principles of guerrilla warfare as the only alternative to build a better world.

With the reading or rereading of *Guerrilla Warfare* you can reach your own conclusions, returning to José Martí's principle of struggling to achieve as much social justice as possible, a principle for which Che fought throughout his revolutionary career.

Harry "Pombo" Villegas

DEDICATION TO CAMILO

This work is dedicated to Camilo Cienfuegos, who should have read and corrected it, but whose fate prevented him from carrying out the task.* These lines and those that follow may be considered a homage of the Rebel Army to its grand captain, to the greatest guerrilla chief that this revolution produced, to an outstanding revolutionary and a fraternal friend.

Camilo was the compañero of a hundred battles, the intimate confidant of Fidel in difficult moments of the war, the stoic fighter who always made sacrifice into an instrument for steeling his own character and forging the morale of his troops.

I believe he would have approved of this manual in which our guerrilla experiences are synthesized, because it is the product of life itself; but he added to the words outlined here the essential vitality of his temperament, his intelligence and his audacity, in such an exact measure as appears in few people in history.

But Camilo should not be seen as an isolated hero performing miraculous feats by virtue of the impulse of his individual genius, but rather as a true product of the people that formed him, as heroes, martyrs, and leaders are always selected through the exigencies of the struggle.

---

* Camilo Cienfuegos was commander of the Antonio Maceo Column No. 2 in the Rebel Army during the Cuban revolutionary war. He was killed in an airplane accident in October 1959.

I don't know if Camilo knew Danton's maxim for revolutionary movements, "Audacity, audacity, and more audacity." Nevertheless, he practiced it in his actions, while adding other qualities necessary in a guerrilla fighter: an ability to assess a situation quickly and precisely and to anticipate problems to be solved in the future.

Although these lines may serve as the homage of the author and of a whole people to our hero, they are not a biography, and do not attempt to relate the many anecdotes about him. Camilo was the subject of a thousand anecdotes; inevitably, he created stories wherever he went. Camilo's easy manner, always appreciated by the people, was matched by a personality that naturally and almost unconsciously put a stamp on everything around him. Few men have succeeded in leaving such a distinctive personal mark on everything they do. As Fidel has said, his culture came not from books; he had the natural intelligence of the people, who had chosen him out of thousands for a privileged place because of the audacity of his strikes, his tenacity, his intelligence, and his unmatched devotion.

Camilo practiced loyalty like a religion; he was a devotee, both in his personal loyalty to Fidel, who embodied the will of the people as no one else, and in his loyalty to the people themselves. The people and Fidel march united, as did the devotions of the invincible guerrilla fighter.

Who killed him?

We should ask instead: Who destroyed his body? Because men like him live on in the people as long as the people will it to be so.

The enemy succeeded in killing him because they wanted him dead; they killed him because there are no safe airplanes; because pilots cannot acquire all the necessary experience; because, overburdened with work, Camilo wished to get back to Havana quickly. And his own character killed him, too. Camilo never calculated danger; he used it as a diversion, he mocked it, lured, toyed, and played with it. In the spirit of a guerrilla fighter a plan could not be postponed on account of a few clouds.

As it was, an entire people had come to know him, admire him, and love him. It might have happened earlier, and his story would be the simple tale of a guerrilla captain. "There will be many Camilos," said Fidel; to that I can add, there were other Camilos, Camilos whose lives ended before completing the magnificent circle that drew Camilo into history. Camilo and the other Camilos (those who did not make it and those who will come after) are the indicators of the power of the people. They are the highest expression of what a nation can produce in a time of war for the defense of its purest ideals, fought with faith in the achievement of its noblest goals.

Let's not typecast him or encase him in a mold — in other words, kill him. Let's leave him there, in general outline, without attributing to him a precise social and economic ideology that was never completely defined. Let's reiterate that there was no other soldier like Camilo in this war of liberation — a complete revolutionary, a man of the people, a product of this revolution that the Cuban nation made for itself. The slightest shadow of weariness or discouragement never entered his head. Camilo, the guerrilla fighter, who made everything "something of Camilo," who put his precise and indelible mark on the Cuban revolution, is a permanent and daily inspiration. He belongs to those others who did not make it and to those who are yet to come.

In his continual and immortal renewal, Camilo is the reflection of the people.

Ernesto Che Guevara

CHAPTER I:
GENERAL PRINCIPLES OF GUERRILLA WARFARE

1 THE ESSENCE OF GUERRILLA WARFARE

The armed victory of the Cuban people over the Batista dictatorship has not only been the triumph of heroism reported by the world's newspapers; it has also forced a change in the old dogmas concerning the conduct of the popular masses of Latin America and clearly demonstrated the capacity of the people to free themselves through guerrilla warfare from an oppressive government.

We consider that the Cuban revolution contributed three fundamental lessons to the revolutionary movements in America.* They are:

1) Popular forces can win a war against the army.

2) It is not always necessary to wait until all the revolutionary conditions exist; the insurrectional *foco*** **can develop subjective conditions based on existing objective conditions.**[1]

3) In underdeveloped America the countryside is the fundamental arena for armed struggle.

Of these three propositions, the first two challenge the defeatist attitude of revolutionaries or inactive pseudo-revolutionaries who take refuge in the argument that against a professional army nothing can be done, and who sit down to wait until

---

* Che uses the word "America" to refer to the Americas, in the tradition of Cuba's national hero, José Martí, who spoke of the continent of Latin America as "Our America."

** *Foco*: a small nucleus of revolutionaries.

1. Most of the changes and additions marked by Che in the original text were written in blue; they are represented in boldface in this edition. Che's use of other colors to make observations or remarks is made clear through footnotes.

all necessary objective and subjective conditions are attained somehow mechanically, without trying to accelerate them. Although now clear to everyone, these two undeniable truths were previously a matter for discussion in Cuba, and are probably still debated **today** in **America.**

Naturally, when speaking of the necessary conditions for a revolution, it should not be assumed they can be created solely through the stimulus of a guerrilla *foco*. It must always be understood that there are minimum **conditions** without which the establishment and consolidation of the *foco* is not practicable. **Moreover,** it is necessary to demonstrate clearly to people the futility of maintaining the fight for social gains within the framework of civil debate. When the oppressive forces maintain themselves in power against the laws **they themselves** established, peace must be considered already broken.[2]

Under these conditions popular discontent expresses itself in more and more active forms, and resistance finally crystallizes, at a given moment, in an outbreak of the **struggle**.

Where a government has come into power through some form of popular vote, fraudulent or not, and maintains at least an appearance of constitutional legality, the guerrilla movement **will experience great difficulties**, as the possibilities for civil struggle have not yet been exhausted.

The third proposition is of a fundamental strategic nature and must be noted by those who dogmatically argue that the mass struggle is based in cities, entirely ignoring the immense weight of the people from the countryside in the life of all the underdeveloped countries of America. This is not to underrate

---

2. There are some parts of the original text that Che proposed to expand on; these are marked in red or green. In this case red was used.

the struggles of the mass of organized workers; but simply to analyze the real possibilities for engaging in armed struggle where the guarantees that usually adorn our constitutions are suspended or ignored. In these conditions the workers' movement must function clandestinely without arms and face enormous dangers. The situation is less difficult in the open countryside, where the armed guerrillas can support the local people, and where there are places beyond the reach of the repressive forces.[3]

Although later we will make a careful analysis, **to begin this task** we want to emphasize three conclusions that are features of the Cuban revolutionary experience and which are fundamental to our argument.

Guerrilla warfare, the basis of the struggle of a people to redeem themselves, has various characteristics, different aspects, even though the essential desire for liberation remains the same. It is obvious — and writers on this theme have said it many times — that war responds to certain <u>laws</u>[4]; and whoever **disregards them** will be defeated. These same laws must rule guerrilla warfare as a phase of war; but because of its special features, a series of corollary <u>laws</u>[5] must also be recognized in order to carry it forward. Although geographical and social conditions in each country determine the mode and particular forms that guerrilla warfare will take, there are general laws that hold for all such struggles.

Our current task is to find the basic principles of this kind of war and the rules to be followed by peoples seeking liberation;

---

3. Ibid.
4. Underlined in green in the original text.
5. In addition to underlining the word in green, in the margin Che wrote in the same color: **See about the laws.**

to develop theory from facts; to generalize and give structure to our experience for the benefit of others.

Let us first consider the question: who are the combatants in a guerrilla war? On one side we have a group composed of the oppressor and his agents, the professional army, well armed and disciplined, in many cases receiving foreign aid as well as the help of the bureaucracy that is beholden to the oppressor. On the other side are the people of the nation or region. It is important to emphasize that guerrilla warfare is a war of the masses, a war of the people. The guerrilla band, as an armed nucleus, is the combative vanguard of the people. Its great force is drawn from the mass of the people themselves. The guerrilla band should not be considered inferior to the army against which it fights simply because it has inferior firepower. Guerrilla warfare is used by the side that is supported by a majority but which possesses a much smaller number of arms for use in defense against oppression.[6]

The guerrilla fighter counts on the full support of the local people. This is an indispensable condition. And this is clearly seen by considering the case of bandit gangs that operate in a region; they have **many** characteristics of a guerrilla army, homogeneity, respect for the leader, bravery, knowledge of the terrain, and, often, even a good understanding of the tactics to be employed. The only thing lacking is the support of the people; and these gangs are inevitably captured and exterminated by the public force.[7]

Analyzing the guerrilla band's mode of operation, its form of struggle, and understanding its mass base, we can answer

---

6. In the margin Che pointed out in red: **Improve editing.**
7. The paragraph appears marked with a vertical green line, and in the same color Che has written: **Delete?**

the question: why does the guerrilla fighter fight? We must come to the inevitable conclusion that the guerrilla fighter is a social reformer, who takes up arms **as the embodiment** of the angry protest of the people against their oppressors; guerrillas fight in order to change the social system that keeps all their unarmed brothers and sisters in ignominy and misery. They launch themselves against the conditions of the ruling institutions at a particular moment and dedicate themselves with all the vigor that circumstances permit to smash the mold of those institutions.

When we analyze more deeply the tactic of guerrilla warfare, we see that guerrilla fighters must have good knowledge of the surrounding countryside; the paths of entry and escape, which will almost always have been constructed by the guerrillas themselves; the possibilities of rapid maneuver; good hiding places; naturally they must also count on the support of the people. All this indicates that the guerrilla fighter will carry out actions in rough, semi-populated areas. Since in such areas the struggle of the people for reforms is aimed primarily and almost exclusively at changing the form of land ownership, the guerrilla fighter is above all an agrarian revolutionary, who interprets the desires of the great peasant mass to be owners of land, owners of their means of production, of their **animals**, of everything they live for, which will also constitute their cemetery.

Current interpretations identify two different types of guerrilla warfare, one of these being a struggle that complements great regular armies, such as was the case of the Ukrainian fighters in the Soviet Union; but this type of warfare will not be considered in this analysis. We are interested in the other type, the case of an armed group engaged in struggle against a constituted power, colonial or otherwise, which establishes itself as a single base and which develops in rural areas. In all such cases, whatever the ideological aims inspiring the struggle, the economic goal is determined by the desire for land.

Mao's China begins as an uprising of groups of workers in the South that is defeated and almost annihilated. It succeeds in establishing itself and begins to advance only after the long march from Yenan, when it bases itself in rural areas and makes agrarian reform its fundamental goal. The struggle of Ho Chi Minh is based among the rice-growing peasants, who are oppressed by the French colonial yoke; with this force it is progressing toward the defeat of the colonialists.[8] In both cases there was the framework of a patriotic war against the Japanese invader, but the economic basis of the fight for land has not disappeared. In the case of Algeria, the grand idea of Arab nationalism has its economic corollary in the fact that a million French settlers utilize nearly all the arable land. In some countries, such as Puerto Rico, where the special conditions of the island have not permitted a guerrilla movement, the nationalist spirit, deeply wounded by daily discrimination, is rooted in the aspiration of the peasants to recover the land that the Yankee invaders seized (even though many of these people are already proletarianized). This same central idea, though in different forms, inspired the small farmers, peasants, and slaves of the eastern estates of Cuba to close ranks and defend the right to possess land during the 30-year war of liberation.*

Considering the possibilities for guerrilla warfare to become transformed into a **conventional** war as the operating potential

---

8. From "In all such cases..." at the end of the previous paragraph, until here, Che has marked the original text in red with vertical lines. He has suggested **fix this**, and then, **expand and improve**.

* The Cuban wars for independence from Spain lasted from 1868 to 1898.

of the guerrilla band increases, this special type of warfare should be considered as an embryo, a prelude, of the other. The possibilities for the growth of the guerrilla band and for changes in the mode of fighting until it becomes conventional warfare are as great as the possibilities for defeating the enemy in each of the different battles, combats, or skirmishes that occur. Therefore, the fundamental principle is that no battle, combat, or skirmish should be fought unless it can be won. There is a pejorative saying: "The guerrilla fighter is the Jesuit of warfare." This suggests qualities of treachery, of surprise, of secretiveness, that are obviously essential elements of guerrilla warfare. Naturally, it is a special kind of Jesuitism, promoted by circumstances, which necessitate acting at certain moments in ways different from the romantic and sporting conceptions with which we are taught to believe war is fought.[9]

War is always a struggle in which each contender tries to annihilate the other. Besides using force, they will have recourse to all kinds of tricks and stratagems in order to achieve this goal. Military strategy and tactics are a representation of the objectives of the groups and of the means of achieving those objectives, taking advantage of all the enemy's weak points. In a war of positions, every platoon in a large army will display the same combative characteristics as those of the guerrilla band: treachery, secretiveness, and surprise. When these are not present, it is because vigilance on the other side prevents surprise. But since the guerrilla band is a division in itself, and since there are large areas of territory not controlled by the enemy, it is always possible to carry out guerrilla attacks in

---

9. From "Naturally, it is a special kind of Jesuitism…" to the end of the paragraph, Che has marked a green line and suggested **fix**.

such a way as to guarantee surprise; and this is what the guerrilla fighter should do.[10]

"Hit and run," some call this scornfully, and this is accurate. Hit and run, wait, lie in ambush, again hit and run, repeatedly, giving the enemy no rest. There would appear in all this a negative quality, an attitude of retreat, of avoiding frontal combat. This is, however, a consequence of the general strategy of guerrilla warfare, the ultimate aim of which is the same as in any war: to win, to annihilate the enemy.

Guerrilla warfare is therefore clearly a phase that does not afford in itself the opportunity to attain a complete victory, but rather is one of the initial phases of a war and will develop continuously until, through steady growth, the guerrilla army acquires the characteristics of a regular army. At that moment it will be ready to deal the enemy definitive blows and to achieve victory. The triumph will always be **achieved by** a regular army, even though its origins were in a guerrilla army.

So, just as the general of a division in a modern war does not have to die in front of his soldiers, the guerrilla fighter, who is the general of himself, need not die in every battle. The guerrilla is ready to give his or her life, but the positive feature of guerrilla warfare is that each guerrilla fighter **is** ready to die not just to defend an idea but to make that idea a reality. That is the essence of the guerrilla struggle. The miracle is that a small nucleus, the armed vanguard of a great popular movement that supports them, can proceed to realize that idea, to establish a new society, to break the old patterns of the past, to achieve, ultimately, the social justice for which they fight.

---

10. From "not controlled by the enemy" to the end of this paragraph, and the entire following paragraph, was marked with a blue line with the note: **Consider the reason for this in the foreword.**

Viewed in this way, what was disparaged acquires true nobility — the nobility of the ends sought, and we are clearly not speaking of a distorted means to an end. This combative attitude, this attitude of never being discouraged, this resolution in confronting the great challenge presented by the final objective also epitomizes the nobility of the guerrilla fighter.

2 GUERRILLA STRATEGY

In the terminology of war, strategy is understood as the analysis of the objectives to be achieved in the light of the total military situation, and the overall ways of accomplishing these objectives.[11]

To have a correct strategic appreciation from the point of view of the guerrilla band, it is necessary to analyze fundamentally the enemy's likely mode of operation. If the final objective is always the complete destruction of the opposing force, in the case of a civil war the enemy is confronted with the standard task: the total destruction of each component of the guerrilla band. The guerrilla fighter, on the other hand, must analyze the resources that the enemy has for trying to achieve that outcome: in terms of men, mobility, popular support, armaments, and the leadership capacity which can be relied on. We must adjust our own strategy on the basis of these considerations, always bearing in mind the final objective of defeating the enemy army.

There are fundamental aspects to be studied: armaments, for example, and how they are used. The value of a tank, of an

---

11. Marked in red with the following observation: **See Clausewitz.** (Carl von Clausewitz (1780–1831) was a Prussian general and military theorist.)

airplane in a fight of this nature must be assessed. The arms of the enemy, his ammunition, his habits must be considered, because the principal source of provision for the guerrilla force is precisely in enemy armaments. If there is a choice, we should choose the same type as that used by the enemy, since the greatest problem of the guerrilla band is the lack of ammunition, which the opponent must provide.

Once objectives have been fixed and analyzed, it is necessary to review the order of the steps leading to the achievement of the final objective. This should be planned in advance, even though it will be modified and adjusted as the struggle develops and unforeseen circumstances arise.

At the outset, the guerrilla fighter's essential task is to keep himself from being wiped out. Step by step, it will become easier for members of the guerrilla band or bands to adapt themselves to their lifestyle and to escape from the forces ranged against them, as this becomes a daily practice. When this is achieved, and it has been able to take up inaccessible positions that **are very difficult** for the enemy to reach, or it has assembled forces that deter the enemy from attacking, the guerrilla band should proceed to the gradual weakening of the enemy. At first, this can be done close to the points of active warfare against the guerrilla band, and later it can be taken deeper into enemy territory, attacking their communications, and then attacking or harassing their bases of operations and their central base, tormenting them wherever possible, to the full extent of the capabilities of the guerrilla forces.

The blows should be continuous. The enemy soldier in a zone of operations should not be allowed to sleep; his outposts should be attacked and destroyed systematically. At every moment the impression should be created that he is completely surrounded. In wooded areas and rough ground this effort should be maintained day and night; in open zones that are more easily penetrated by enemy patrols, only at night. For this, the absolute cooperation of the people and a perfect knowledge of the terrain are necessary. These two conditions affect every minute of the guerrilla fighter's life. Therefore, along with centers for the study of current and future zones of operations, intensive work must be undertaken among the local people to explain the motives of the revolution, its goals, and to spread the incontrovertible truth that the enemy's victory over the people is ultimately impossible. *Whoever does not feel this indisputable truth cannot be a guerrilla fighter.*

To begin with, this work among the people should be aimed at ensuring secrecy; that is, each peasant, each member of the community in which the action is taking place, will be asked not to mention what he or she sees and hears; later, help can be sought from those local residents whose loyalty to the revolution offers greater guarantees; later on, these persons can be used in contact missions, to transport goods or arms, or as guides in the zones familiar to them; after that, it is possible to establish organized mass action in workplaces, of which the final result will be the general strike.[12]

The strike is a most important element in a civil war, but in order to achieve it a range of complementary conditions are necessary that do not always exist, and which very rarely emerge spontaneously. These fundamental conditions must be created, basically by explaining the purpose of the revolution and by demonstrating the power of the people and their capabilities.

---

12. The end of this paragraph from "organized mass action" and the entire following paragraph were marked with a vertical green line with the note: **Correct this in accordance with the Vietnamese [experience].**

It is also possible to have recourse to certain very homogeneous groups, which must have shown their efficacy previously in less dangerous tasks, in order to make use of sabotage, another of the terrible arms of the guerrilla band. Entire armies can be paralyzed, the industrial life of a zone suspended, leaving the inhabitants of a city without factories, without light, without water, without communications of any kind, without being able to risk travel by road except at certain times. If all this is achieved, the morale of the enemy declines, the morale of combatant units weakens, and the fruit ripens for picking at the precise moment.

All this presupposes an extension of the territory in which the guerrilla action takes place, but an excessive increase of this territory should be avoided. A strong base of operations must always be preserved and continuously strengthened during the course of the war. Within this territory, the indoctrination* of local residents should take place; the irreconcilable enemies of the revolution should be quarantined; all simple defensive measures, such as trenches, mines, and communications, should be perfected.

When the guerrilla band has achieved a respectable level of armed power in terms of arms and the number of combatants, it should proceed to the formation of new columns. This is similar to the beehive that at a particular moment releases a new queen, who goes off to another region with a part of the swarm. The mother hive with the most outstanding guerrilla chief will stay in the less dangerous places, while the new columns will penetrate other enemy territories following the cycle already described.

---

* Che uses the term "indoctrination" to mean political education.

The time will come when the territory occupied by the columns is too small for them; and in advancing toward regions strongly defended by the enemy, it will be necessary to confront powerful forces. At that moment the columns combine to offer a compact fighting front, and a war of positions commences, a war conducted by regular armies. Nevertheless, the former guerrilla army cannot cut itself off from its base, and should create new guerrilla bands operating behind the enemy lines as the original bands did, proceeding in this way to penetrate enemy territory until it is controlled.

This is how the guerrillas reach the stage of attack, of the encirclement of fortified bases, of the defeat of reinforcements, of mass action, ever more committed, throughout the entire national territory, finally accomplishing the objective of the war: victory.

3 GUERRILLA TACTICS

In military terms, tactics are the practical methods of achieving great strategic objectives.

In one sense, they complement strategy, and in another they are more specific rules within it. As a means to an end, tactics are much more variable, much more flexible than the final objectives, and they should be adjusted continually during the struggle. There are tactical objectives that remain constant throughout a war and others that vary. The first thing to be considered is the adjusting of guerrilla operations to the enemy's actions.[13]

---

13. The two first paragraphs of this section are marked in red, with the note: **See Clausewitz.**

The fundamental characteristic of a guerrilla band is mobility. Within a few minutes it can move away from a specific theatre and in a few hours farther still from the region, if that becomes necessary; this mobility allows the guerrillas to constantly change fronts and avoid any kind of encirclement. As circumstances of the war permit, the guerrilla band can dedicate itself exclusively to fleeing from an encirclement, which is the enemy's only way of forcing it into a decisive encounter that might be unfavorable; it can also change the battle into a counter-encirclement (small groups of guerrillas are assumed to be surrounded by the enemy when suddenly the enemy itself is surrounded by stronger contingents; or men positioned in a safe place serve as a lure, leading to the encirclement and annihilation of the entire troop and supply of the attacking force). A feature of this mobile war is the "minuet," so named for its similarity to the dance: the guerrilla bands encircle an enemy position, such as an advancing column; it is surrounded completely from the four points of the compass,[14] with five or six guerrillas at each point, far enough away to avoid being encircled themselves; the battle is started at any one of the points, and the army moves toward it; the guerrillas then retreat, always maintaining visual contact, and initiate an attack from another point. The army will repeat its action and the guerrilla band the same. Thus, successively, an enemy column can be kept immobilized, and forced to expend large quantities of ammunition, weakening the morale of its troops at no great risk to the guerrillas.

This same tactic can be applied at night, but closing in more and showing greater aggression, because in these conditions counter-encirclement is much more difficult. Movement by

---

14. From "A feature of this mobile war…" to here, Che has marked in red with the observation: **Correct this**.

night is another important trait of the guerrilla band, enabling it to advance into an attack position and to organize in a new territory where the danger of betrayal might exist. The numerical inferiority of the guerrilla band makes it necessary that attacks are always carried out by surprise; this is the great advantage that allows the guerrillas to inflict losses on the enemy without suffering losses themselves. In a battle between 100 men on one side and 10 on the other, the losses are not equal if there is one casualty on each side. The enemy loss can always be overcome, representing only one percent of their effective forces. A loss for the guerrilla band requires more time to be replaced as it involves a highly specialized soldier and represents 10 percent of the operating forces.

Dead guerrilla soldiers should never be left with their arms and ammunition. The duty of every guerrilla fighter, whenever a compañero falls, is to recover immediately these extremely precious elements of struggle. Specifically, the care that must be taken of ammunition and the method of using it are other characteristics of guerrilla warfare. In any combat between a regular force and a guerrilla band it is always possible to distinguish one from the other by their different manner of fire: a regular army will use a great deal of firepower, the guerrillas' shots will be sporadic and accurate.

At one time, one of our heroes, now dead, had to employ his machine gun for nearly five minutes, burst after burst, in order to slow the advance of enemy soldiers. This caused considerable confusion in our forces, because they assumed from the rhythm of fire that that key position must have been taken by the enemy; this was one of the rare occasions where a departure from the rule of saving fire had been necessary because of the importance of the position being defended.

Another elementary characteristic of the guerrilla soldier is flexibility, an ability to adapt to any circumstance, and to convert all accidents of the action to advantage. Contrary to the rigidity of classical methods of war, guerrilla fighters invent their own tactics at every minute of the battle and constantly surprise the enemy.

In the first case, there are only elastic positions, specific places that the enemy cannot pass, and places of diverting him. After easily overcoming difficulties in a gradual advance, the enemy is frequently surprised to find himself suddenly and solidly caught with no possibility of moving forward. This is because, when they have been selected on the basis of a careful study of the terrain, the guerrilla-defended positions are **almost** invulnerable. It is not the number of attacking soldiers that counts, but the number of defending soldiers. Once that number is in position, it can **nearly always** successfully hold off a battalion. It is a major task of the chiefs to choose carefully the timing and the place for defending a position without retreat.

The form of attack of a guerrilla army is also different; starting with surprise and ferocity, implacable, it suddenly converts itself into total passivity. The surviving enemy, resting, believes that the attacker has left; he begins to relax, to return to routine life within the **besieged position**, when suddenly a new attack bursts forth in another place, with the same characteristics, while the main body of the guerrilla band lies in wait to intercept reinforcements. **At other times** the guerrillas will suddenly attack an outpost defending the camp, overwhelm and capture it. The fundamental thing is surprise and rapidity of attack.

Acts of sabotage are very important. A clear distinction must be made between sabotage, a revolutionary and highly effective method of warfare, and terrorism, a measure that is generally ineffective and indiscriminate in its results, since it often makes victims of innocent people and destroys many lives that would be valuable to the revolution. Terrorism should be considered a valuable tactic when it is used to put to death some noted leader of the oppressive forces who is known for his cruelty, his efficiency in repression, or for another reason that makes his elimination useful. But the killing of insignificant individuals is never advisable, since it results in increased reprisals, and inevitable deaths.

There is one very controversial point about terrorism. Many consider that by provoking police oppression, it hinders all more or less legal or semi-clandestine contact with the masses and makes impossible the united action that might be necessary at a critical moment. This is true; but in a civil war the repression by the governmental power in certain towns might **already** be so great that, in fact, all forms of legal action are suppressed, and any mass action that is not supported by arms is ruled out. Therefore, it is necessary to be circumspect in adopting methods of this nature and to assess the general favorable consequences for the revolution.[15] At any rate, well-managed sabotage is always a very effective weapon. It should not be used to immobilize means of production, which would paralyze a sector of the population (in other words, leave them unemployed), unless this also affects the normal life of the society. Sabotage against a soft-drink factory is ridiculous, but sabotage against a power plant is absolutely correct and advisable. In the first instance, a certain number of workers are put out of work without disrupting the rhythm of industry; in the second case, there will also be displaced workers, but this is entirely justified by the paralysis of regional life. We will return to the technique of sabotage later.

---

15. Che proposes **improve**, in red.

Aviation is one of the favorite weapons of a **conventional** army in modern times, supposedly a decisive one. Nevertheless, it is useless during the early phases of a guerrilla war, when there are only small concentrations of guerrillas in rugged places. The effectiveness of aviation is in its systematic destruction of visible and organized defenses; and for this there must be large concentrations of men who construct these defenses, something nonexistent in warfare of this nature. Planes are also potent against **marches by columns** on level ground or places **without** cover; however, this vulnerability can be easily avoided by conducting marches at night.

One of the enemy's weakest points is road and rail transportation. It is virtually impossible to guard every meter of a transport route, a road, or a railroad. At any point a considerable amount of explosives can be planted that will make the road impassable; and by detonating explosives when a vehicle passes by, besides cutting off the road, considerable loss of life and materiel can be inflicted on the enemy.

The sources of explosives are varied: they can be brought from other zones; or unexploded bombs **dropped from enemy planes** can be used, although these do not always work; or they can be manufactured in secret laboratories within the guerrilla zone. The techniques of detonation are quite varied; their manufacture also depends on the conditions of the guerrilla band.[16]

In our laboratory we made powder that we used as a cap, and we invented various devices for exploding mines at the desired moment. Those that produced the best results were electric, but the first mine we exploded was a bomb dropped from a plane

---

16. Che proposes **improve,** in red.

of the [Batista] dictatorship; we adapted it by inserting various caps and adding a gun with the trigger pulled by a cord. At the moment an enemy truck passed, the weapon was fired to set off the explosion.

These techniques can be developed to a high degree. For example, we have learned that in Algeria today, in the struggle against the French colonial power, they are using tele-explosive mines, that is, mines exploded by radio at great distances from the point where they are located.[17]

The tactic of setting up ambushes along roads in order to explode mines and annihilate survivors is one of the most profitable for obtaining arms and ammunition. The surprised enemy cannot use their ammunition and has no time to flee; so with a small expenditure of ammunition significant results are achieved. As the enemy receives blows, they also change their tactics, and instead of isolated trucks, moves in veritable motorized columns. However, by choosing the terrain well, the same result can be produced by breaking up the column and concentrating forces on one vehicle. In these cases the essential elements of guerrilla tactics must always be kept in mind. These are: perfect knowledge of the area; surveillance and foresight as to the lines of escape; vigilance over all the secondary roads that might bring in reinforcements to the point of attack; intimacy with people in the zone so as to ensure their help in regard to supplies, transport, and temporary or permanent hiding places if it becomes necessary to leave wounded compañeros behind; numerical superiority at a chosen point of action; total mobility; and the possibility of counting on reserves.

If all these basic tactics are employed, surprise attacks

---

17. Marked in red with the note: **Correct.**

along the enemy's lines of communication yield important dividends.

A fundamental part of guerrilla tactics is the treatment of the people in the zone. The treatment of the enemy is similarly important; the norm should be absolute inflexibility during attack, an absolute inflexibility toward all the contemptible elements that resort to informing and assassination, and the **greatest** clemency **possible** toward the enemy soldiers who go into battle performing — or believing that they are performing — their military duty. It is a good policy to take no prisoners while there are no significant operational bases and no unassailable positions. Survivors should be set free. The wounded should be cared for with all available resources at the time of the action. Conduct toward the civil population should be governed by great respect for all the customs and traditions of the people of the zone, in order to demonstrate effectively, through deeds, the moral superiority of the guerrilla fighter over the **oppressing** soldier.

4 WARFARE ON FAVORABLE TERRAIN

As already stated, the guerrilla struggle will not always take place on the most favorable terrain for the employment of its tactics; but when it does, that is, when the guerrilla band is located in zones difficult to reach, either because of dense forests, steep mountains, or impassable deserts or marshes, the general tactics, based on the fundamental postulates of guerrilla warfare, must always be the same.

An important point to consider is the way to engage the enemy. If the zone is so dense, so difficult that an organized army can never reach it, the guerrilla band should advance to the regions where the army can get to and where there are possibilities for combat.

The guerrilla band should fight as soon as its survival has been assured; it must constantly leave its refuge to fight; it does not have to be as mobile as in those cases where the terrain is unfavorable; it must adjust itself to the conditions of the enemy, but is not required to move as quickly as in those areas where the enemy can concentrate a large number of men in a few minutes. Neither is the nocturnal character of this warfare so important; it will be possible in many cases to carry out daytime operations, especially mobilizations by day, though subjected to enemy observation by land and air. It is also possible to **pursue** military **action** for a much longer time, above all in the mountains; it is possible to undertake battles of long duration with very few guerrillas, and it is very probable that the arrival of enemy reinforcements at the field of battle can be prevented.

A close vigilance over the access points is, however, an axiom never to be forgotten by guerrilla fighters. Their aggressiveness (on account of the difficulties that the enemy faces in bringing in reinforcements) can be greater, they can get closer to the enemy, fight much more directly, more frontally and for a longer time, although all of this may be qualified by various factors, for example, such as the amount of ammunition.

Fighting on favorable terrain, particularly in the mountains, presents many advantages but also the inconvenience that it is difficult in a single operation to capture a large quantity of arms and ammunition, owing to the precautions that the enemy takes in these areas. (The guerrilla soldier must never forget the fact that the enemy must serve as the source of arms and ammunition.) The guerrilla band will be able to "dig in" here much more rapidly than on unfavorable ground, that is, to form a base from which to engage in a war of positions, where small industries may be established as they are needed, as well as hospitals, centers for education and training, storage facilities, propaganda organs, etc., adequately protected from aircraft or from long-range artillery.

In these conditions the guerrilla band can expand its numbers, including noncombatants and perhaps even a system of training in the use of those arms that eventually fall into the hands of the guerrilla army.

The size of a guerrilla band is extremely flexible, depending on the territory, the means available of obtaining supplies, the flight of oppressed people from other zones, the arms available, and the necessities of organization. But, in any case, it is far more practicable to establish a base and expand with the support of new combatant elements.

This type of guerrilla band's radius of action will be as wide as conditions or the operations of other bands in adjacent territory permit.[18] The range will be restricted by the time it takes to reach a secure zone from the zone of operations; assuming that marches must be made at night, it is not possible to operate more than five or six hours away from a point of maximum security. Small guerrilla bands that work constantly at weakening a territory can go farther from the security zone.

For this type of warfare the preferred arms are long-range weapons requiring minimal expenditure of bullets, supported by a group of automatic or semi-automatic arms. Of the rifles and machine guns available in the US markets, one of the best is the M-1 rifle, called the Garand.[19] This should, however, only be used by those with some experience, since it has the

---

18. Marked in red with the note: **Fix.**
19. Using the color red, Che suggests **improve**.

disadvantage of expending too much ammunition. Medium-heavy arms, such as tripod machine guns, can be used on favorable ground, affording a greater margin of security for the weapon and its personnel, but they **will** always **be** weapons of defense and **not** of attack.

An ideal composition for a guerrilla band of 25 fighters would be 10 to 15 **single-shot** rifles and about 10 automatic arms between Garands and hand machine guns, including light and easily portable automatic arms such as the Browning or the more modern Belgian FAL and M-14 automatic rifles. Nine-millimeter weapons are among the best hand machine guns because they carry more ammunition. The simpler the construction, the better, because this increases the chance of being able to replace parts. All this depends on the armaments the enemy uses, since the ammunition they have is what we will use when their arms fall into our hands. Heavy arms are practically impossible to use. Aircraft cannot see anything in these zones and cease to operate; tanks and cannons cannot do much because of the difficulties of advancing.

A very important consideration is supply. For this very reason, remote zones generally present special problems, since there are few peasants and thus animal and food supplies are scarce. Stable lines of communication must be maintained in order to be able always to rely on a minimum of stockpiled food in the event of any unfortunate contingency.

In this kind of operational zone there are generally no possibilities for sabotage on a large scale; the inaccessibility brings a lack of installations, telephone lines, aqueducts, etc., that could be damaged by direct action.

Animals are important for supply purposes, the mule being the best option in rough country. Adequate pasturage permitting good nutrition is essential. The mule can manage in extremely hilly country impossible for other animals. In the most difficult situations it may be necessary to resort to transport by men. Each individual can carry 25 kilograms for many hours a day and for many days.

The lines of communication with the outside should include a series of intermediate points staffed by totally reliable people, where goods can be stored and where contacts can be hidden at critical times. Internal lines of communication can also be created; their extension will depend on the stage of development reached by the guerrilla band. In some zones of operations in the recent Cuban [revolutionary] war, many kilometers of telephone lines were established, roads were built, and a messenger service was maintained sufficient to cover all areas in minimal time.

There are also other possible means of outside communication we did not use in the Cuban war but which are perfectly appropriate, such as smoke signals, signals using light reflected by mirrors, and carrier pigeons.[20]

For the guerrillas it is of vital importance to maintain their arms in good condition, to capture ammunition, and, above all, to have adequate shoes. The first efforts to create industries should therefore be directed toward meeting these needs. Shoe factories can initially be cobbler workshops that can replace half-soles on old shoes, later developing into various organized factories producing a good daily average of shoes. The manufacture of powder is fairly simple, and a lot can be

---

20. Che marked this paragraph for deletion, and noted in red: **Radio**, perhaps as an element to expand on in future corrections. Radio broadcasts were well utilized by the Rebel Army in Cuba, and in Chapter III, in the section on propaganda, Che describes the role of radio in the development of the struggle.

accomplished with a small laboratory, bringing in the necessary materials from outside. Mines constitute a grave danger for the enemy; large areas can be mined for simultaneous explosion, destroying up to hundreds of men.[21]

5 WARFARE ON UNFAVORABLE TERRAIN

To conduct warfare in territory that is not particularly hilly, lacks forests, and has many roads, all the fundamentals of guerrilla warfare must be observed, with only the forms altered. The quantity, not the quality, of guerrilla warfare will change. For example, following the same order as before, the mobility of this type of guerrilla band should be extraordinary; strikes should preferably be made at night; they should be extremely rapid, almost explosive, and the guerrillas should then withdraw to a different place from their starting point, as far as possible from the scene of the action, assuming that there is no place secure from the repressive forces that the guerrillas can use as their garrison.

A guerrilla can walk between 30 and 50 kilometers during the night; marching is also possible during the first hours of daylight, unless the operational zones are closely watched or there is a danger that local people will see the passing troops and notify the pursuing army of the guerrilla band's location and route. In these cases it is always preferable to operate at night, keeping as quiet as possible both before and after the action; the first hours of darkness are best. Here too there are exceptions to the general rule, as sometimes dawn might be

---

21. Che proposes to **improve** the end of the paragraph, in red.

preferable. It is never wise to let the enemy get used to a certain form of warfare; it is necessary to vary constantly the places, the hours, and the forms of operation.

We have already said that the action cannot be for long, but must be rapid; it must be highly effective, last a few minutes, and be followed by an immediate withdrawal. The arms employed here will not be the same as in the case of actions on favorable ground; a large quantity of automatic weapons is preferable. In night attacks marksmanship is not the determining factor, but rather concentrated fire; the more automatic arms firing at short distance, the more possibilities there are of annihilating the enemy.

Furthermore, the mining of roads and the destruction of bridges are tactics of great importance. Guerrilla attacks will be less aggressive so far as perseverance and duration are concerned, but they can be very violent, and they can utilize different arms, such as mines and the shotgun. Against open vehicles heavily loaded with soldiers — the usual method of transporting troops — and even against closed vehicles that do not have special defenses or against buses, for example, the shotgun is a tremendous weapon. A shotgun loaded with large shot is the most effective. This is not a secret of guerrilla warfare but is used also in major wars; the North Americans used shotgun platoons armed with high-quality weapons and bayonets for assaulting machine-gun nests.

An important problem to explain is that of ammunition; this will almost always be taken from the enemy. It is therefore necessary to strike where there is the absolute guarantee of replacing whatever ammunition is expended, unless there are large reserves in secure places. In other words, a devastating attack against a group of men should not be undertaken at the risk of expending all ammunition without being able to replace it. In guerrilla tactics it is always necessary to keep in mind the grave problem of procuring the war materiel required to continue the fight. For this reason guerrilla arms should be the same as those of the enemy, except for weapons such as revolvers and shotguns, for which ammunition can be obtained locally or in the cities.

The number of people in a guerrilla band of this type should not exceed 10 to 15. In establishing a single combat unit it is of utmost importance to always consider the limitations on numbers: 10, 12, 15 guerrillas can hide anywhere and at the same time can help each other in putting up a powerful resistance to the enemy. Four or five would perhaps be too small a number, but when the number exceeds 10 there is a greater possibility that the enemy will discover them in their camp or on the march.

Remember that the pace of the guerrilla band on the march is equal to the pace of its slowest person. It is more difficult to achieve a uniform marching speed with 20, 30, or 40 guerrillas than with 10. And on the plains, the guerrilla fighter must essentially be a runner. There the practice of hitting and running is most useful. The guerrilla bands on the plains suffer the enormous disadvantage of being subject to rapid encirclement and of not having secure places where they can set up a firm resistance; they must therefore live in conditions of absolute secrecy for a long time, since it would be dangerous to trust any local person whose fidelity is not perfectly established. Enemy reprisals are so violent, usually so brutal, inflicted not only on the head of the family but frequently on the women and children as well, that pressure on individuals lacking firmness may result at any moment in capitulation and their revealing information as to where the guerrilla band is located and how it is operating. This would immediately result in encirclement, with the inevitable unfortunate consequences, although not necessarily fatal ones. When conditions, the quantity of arms, and the rebelliousness of the people demand an increase in the number of fighters, the guerrilla band should be divided. If necessary, all can regroup at a particular moment to deal a blow, but in such a way that immediately afterwards they can disperse toward separate zones, again divided into small groups of 10, 12, or 15.

Entire armies can be organized under a single command and respect and obedience assured to this command without the necessity of being in a single group. Therefore, the election of the guerrilla chiefs and the certainty that they coordinate ideologically and personally with the overall chief of the zone are very important.

The bazooka is a heavy weapon that can be used by the guerrilla band because of its easy portability and operation. Today the rifle-fired anti-tank grenade can replace it. Naturally, it will be a weapon taken from the enemy. The bazooka is ideal for firing on armored vehicles, and even on unarmored vehicles that are loaded with troops, and for seizing small military bases of just a few men in a short time; but it is important to point out that a man can only carry three shells, and even this requires considerable exertion.[22]

As for using the heavy arms taken from the enemy, naturally nothing should be scorned; but there are weapons such as the tripod machine gun, the heavy 50-millimeter machine gun, etc., which, when captured, should be utilized on the understanding

---

22. At the bottom of the page Che wrote in red: **"This is the experience with US shells for bazookas of ...mm. In other types the load can change."** The number of millimeters is blank in the original.

that they might be lost again. In other words, in the unfavorable conditions that we are now considering, a battle to defend a heavy machine gun or other weapon of this type cannot be allowed; they should simply be used until the tactical moment when they must be abandoned. In our Cuban war of liberation, to abandon a weapon constituted a grave offense, and there was never a case where it was necessary. Nevertheless, we mention this in order to explain clearly the only situation in which abandonment would not be such a critical offense. On unfavorable ground, the guerrilla's weapon is the personal weapon of rapid fire.

A peasant population will usually inhabit an accessible zone, and this enormously facilitates supply. Having trustworthy people and making contact with establishments that provide supplies to the population, it is possible to maintain a guerrilla band perfectly without having to devote time or money to long and dangerous lines of communication. Furthermore, it is well to reiterate that the smaller the number of guerrillas, the easier it will be to provide them with food. Essential supplies such as bedding, waterproof material, mosquito nets, shoes, medicines, and food can be found within the zone, since these are items used daily by the local population.

Communications will be much easier in the sense of being able to count on a larger number of guerrillas and more roads; but they will be more difficult in regard to the security necessary for sending messages between distant points, since it will be necessary to rely on a range of contacts that have to be trustworthy. There will be the danger of an eventual capture of one of the messengers, who are constantly crossing enemy lines. If the messages are not so important, they should be verbal; if of great importance, writing in code should be used. Experience shows that transmission by word of mouth greatly distorts any communication.

For these same reasons industry will have much less importance, as well as being much more difficult to carry out. It will not be possible to have factories making shoes or arms. Practically speaking, industry will have to be limited to small workshops, carefully hidden, where shotgun shells can be recharged and mines, simple grenades, and other bare necessities of the moment manufactured. On the other hand, it is possible to make use of all the friendly local workshops to make whatever is necessary.

This brings us to two consequences that flow logically from what has been said. First, the favorable conditions for establishing a permanent camp in guerrilla warfare determine the degree of productive development of a particular location. All favorable conditions, all the comforts of life usually induce people to settle down; but the opposite is the case for the guerrilla band. The more facilities there are for social life, the more nomadic, the less certain the life of the guerrilla fighter. In reality, this is the result of one and the same principle. The title of this section is "Warfare on Unfavorable Terrain," because everything that is favorable to human life: communications, urban and semi-urban concentrations of large numbers of people, land easily worked by machine — all these place the guerrilla fighter in a disadvantaged position.

The second conclusion is that as guerrilla warfare must necessarily include the extremely important factor of work among the masses, this task is even more important in the unfavorable zones, where a single enemy attack can produce a catastrophe. Indoctrination should be constant, as should be the struggle for unity of the workers, the peasants, and other social classes that live in the zone, in order to achieve the greatest homogeneous attitude toward the guerrillas. This task with the masses, this continuous attention to the huge problem of relations between the guerrilla band and the local residents, must also govern the attitude taken toward the case of an individual recalcitrant enemy soldier: he should be eliminated without hesitation if he is a danger. In this respect the guerrilla band must be severe. Enemies cannot be permitted to exist within the operational zone that offers no security.

6 URBAN WARFARE

If, during the war, the guerrilla bands move in on the cities and penetrate the surrounding countryside in such a way as to be able to create conditions of some security, it will be necessary to give these urban bands special education, or rather, a special organization.

It is essential to recognize that an urban guerrilla band can never emerge of its own accord.[23] It will be born only after certain conditions necessary for its survival have been created. Therefore, the urban guerrilla will always be under the direct command of chiefs located in another zone. The function of this guerrilla band will not be to carry out independent actions but to coordinate its activities with the overall strategic **plans** in such a way as to support the action of larger groups situated in another area, contributing specifically to the success of a particular tactical objective, without the operational freedom of other types of guerrilla bands. For example, an urban band

---

23. Che proposes **improve**, in red.

will not be able to choose the nature of its operation: whether to destroy telephone lines, to make attacks in another locality, or to surprise a patrol of soldiers on a distant road; it will do exactly what it is told. If its function is to cut down telephone poles or electric wires, to destroy sewers, railroads, or water mains, it will limit itself to carrying out these tasks efficiently.

It should not number more than four or five. The limitation on numbers is important, because the urban guerrilla must be considered as operating on exceptionally unfavorable terrain, where the enemy's vigilance will be much greater and the possibilities of reprisals as well as of betrayal are increased enormously. Another aggravating factor is that the urban guerrilla band cannot go far from the places where it is going to operate; added to speedy action and withdrawal there is also a limit on the distance of withdrawal from the scene of action and the need to remain totally hidden during the daytime. This is a nocturnal guerrilla band in the extreme, with no possibility to change its mode of operation until it can take part **as an** active combatant in the siege of the city when the insurrection is very advanced.

The essential qualities of the guerrilla fighter in this unfavorable situation are discipline — perhaps to the highest degree — and discretion. No more than two or three friendly houses can be relied on to provide food; it is almost certain that an encirclement under these conditions equals death. Besides, weapons will not be the same kind as those used by other groups. They will be for personal defense, only those that do not hinder a rapid flight or betray a secure hiding place. The group should have not more than one or two **sawed-off automatic weapons**, with **pistols** for the other members.

Preferably they will concentrate on prescribed sabotage

actions and never carry out armed attacks, except by surprising one or two members or agents of the enemy troops.

For this they need a broad range of equipment. The guerrilla fighter must have good saws, large quantities of dynamite, picks and shovels, apparatus for lifting rails, and, in general, adequate tools for the work to be carried out. These should be hidden in places that are secure but easily accessible to those who will need them.

If there is more than one guerrilla band, they will depend on a single chief to give orders as to the necessary tasks through contacts of proven trustworthiness that live openly as ordinary citizens. In certain cases guerrilla fighters will be able to maintain their peacetime work, but this is very difficult; practically speaking, the urban guerrilla band is **constituted by** a group of individuals who are already outside the **law**, in a situation of war, in unfavorable conditions as already described.

The importance of the urban struggle is **extraordinary**. A good operation of this nature extended over a wide area can almost completely paralyze the commercial and industrial life of the sector and place the entire population in a situation of unrest, of anguish, almost of impatience for the development of violent events that will relieve the suspense. If, from the moment war is initiated, the future possibility of such a struggle is anticipated and organization of specialists in this field commences, much more rapid action can be guaranteed and lives and precious time will be saved.

CHAPTER II:
THE GUERRILLA BAND

1 THE GUERRILLA FIGHTER: SOCIAL REFORMER

We have already identified the guerrilla fighter as one who shares the longing of the people for liberation and who, after peaceful means are exhausted, initiates the struggle and converts himself into an armed vanguard of the fighting people. From the commencement of the struggle the guerrilla is committed to destroying an unjust order and has the intention, more or less hidden, to replace the old with something new.

We have also said that in the current conditions, at least in America and in almost all countries with little economic development, the countryside offers ideal conditions for the struggle, thus the basic social claims that the guerrilla fighter will raise begin with changes in the structure of agrarian property.

In this period the banner of the struggle will be agrarian reform. At first this goal may or may not be completely defined in its extent and limits; it may simply refer to the age-old hunger of the peasant for the land he or she works or wishes to work.

The conditions in which the agrarian reform will be realized depend on the conditions that existed before the struggle began, and on the social depth of the struggle. But the guerrilla fighter, as the conscious element of the vanguard of the people, must display the moral conduct of a true priest of the desired reform. To the stoicism forced by the difficult conditions of warfare should be added an austerity born of rigid self-control that prevents a single excess, a single slip, whatever the circumstances. The guerrilla soldier should be an ascetic.[1]

---

1. Marked in red with the note: **Move this section**. It is not specified where it should be moved.

Social relations will vary according to the development of the war. At the beginning it will not be possible to attempt any changes in the social order of the area.

Goods that cannot be paid for in cash will be paid for with bonds; and these should be redeemed at the first opportunity.

The peasant must always be given technical, economic, moral, and cultural assistance. The guerrilla fighter will be a kind of guardian angel who has dropped into the zone, always helping the poor and harassing the rich as little as possible in the first phases of the war. But as the war develops, contradictions will become sharper; the time will arrive when many of those who regarded the revolution sympathetically at the start will place themselves in a position diametrically opposed to it; and they will make the first move into battle against the popular forces. At that moment the guerrilla fighter should act to become the standard-bearer of the people's cause, punishing every betrayal with justice. Private property should acquire a social function in the war zones. In other words, excess land and livestock not essential for the maintenance of a wealthy family should pass into the hands of the people and be distributed equitably and fairly.

The right of the owners to receive payment for possessions used for the social good should always be respected; but this payment will be made in bonds ("bonds of hope," as they were called by our teacher, General Bayo,* referring to the common interest that is thus established between debtor and creditor).

The land and property of notorious and active enemies of the revolution should pass immediately into the hands of the

---

* General Alberto Bayo was a Cuban veteran of the Spanish Civil War, who helped train Fidel Castro's force in Mexico before they returned to Cuba in December 1956 to initiate the guerrilla war in the Sierra Maestra.

revolutionary forces. Furthermore, taking advantage of the heat of the war — those moments in which human fraternity reaches its greatest intensity — all kinds of **cooperative** work should be stimulated, as far as the mentality of the local people will allow.

As social reformers, guerrilla fighters should not only provide an example in their own lives, but should also constantly give an orientation on ideological issues, explaining what they know and what they wish to do at the right time. They should also make use of what they learn as the months or years of the war strengthen their revolutionary convictions, making them more radical as the potency of arms is demonstrated, as the outlook of the local people becomes a part of their spirit and of their own life, and as they understand the justice and the vital necessity of many changes, the theoretical importance of which they understood before, but perhaps not the practical urgency.

Very often this occurs because the initiators of a guerrilla war, or rather the directors of guerrilla warfare, are not those who have bent their backs day after day over the furrow. They understand the necessity for change in the social treatment of the peasants, but have never suffered this bitter treatment personally. What happens then (here, I am drawing on the Cuban experience and expanding on it) is a genuine interaction between those leaders, who by their actions teach the people the fundamental importance of the armed struggle, and the people themselves, who rise in rebellion and teach the leaders these practical necessities we are discussing. In this way, as a product of the interaction between the guerrilla fighters and their people, a progressive radicalization appears, further accentuating the revolutionary nature of the movement and giving it a national scope.

2 THE GUERRILLA FIGHTER AS COMBATANT

The life and activities of the guerrilla fighter, as sketched in general outline, demand a range of physical, mental, and moral qualities needed for adapting oneself to prevailing conditions and for completely fulfilling any assigned mission.

To the question of what the guerrilla soldier should be like, the first answer is that he or she should preferably be an inhabitant of the zone. If this is the case, they will have friends who will help; as a local resident, they will know the area (and this knowledge of the terrain is one of the most important factors in guerrilla warfare); and since they will be accustomed to local peculiarities they will be able to work better, not to mention that they will add to all this the enthusiasm that arises from defending one's own people and struggling to change a social regime that affects one's own world.

The guerrilla combatant is a night combatant; to say this also means to say that he or she must have all the special qualities that such a struggle requires. The guerrilla must be cunning and able to march to combat across plains or mountains without detection, and then to fall on the enemy, taking advantage of the factor of surprise, which must be emphasized again as so important in this type of fight. After causing panic by this surprise, the guerrillas should launch themselves implacably into the fight, never permitting a single weakness in their compañeros and taking advantage of every sign of weakness on the enemy's part. Striking like a tornado, destroying everything, giving no quarter unless the tactical circumstances demand it, judging those who must be judged, sowing panic among the enemy combatants, the guerrillas nevertheless treat defenseless prisoners benevolently and show respect for the dead.

A wounded enemy should be treated with care and respect unless his former life warrants the death penalty, in which case he will be treated according to his deserts. Prisoners can never be kept unless a secure base of operations, invulnerable to the enemy, has been established. Otherwise, the prisoner will become a dangerous menace to the security of the local people of the region or to the guerrilla band itself, because of the information that he can give on rejoining the enemy army. If he has not been a notorious criminal, he should be set free after receiving a lecture.[2]

Guerrilla fighters should risk their lives whenever necessary and be ready to die without hesitation; but, at the same time, they should be cautious and never expose themselves unnecessarily. All possible precautions should be taken to avoid defeat or annihilation. For this reason it is extremely important in every battle to maintain vigilance over all the points from which enemy reinforcements may arrive and to take precautions against encirclement, the consequences of which are usually not physically disastrous but which damage morale by causing a loss of faith in the prospects of the struggle.

Nevertheless, the guerrilla fighter should be audacious, and after carefully analyzing the dangers and possibilities in an action, always ready to take an optimistic attitude toward circumstances and to see reasons for a favorable outcome even at times when the analysis of the adverse and favorable conditions does not appear to be positive.

To be able to survive in the midst of these conditions of struggle and enemy action, guerrilla fighters must have a degree of adaptability that allows them to identify themselves with the

---

2. Che suggests in red: **Move this section**, without specifying where to.

environment in which they live, to become a part of it, and to take advantage of it as an ally to the greatest possible extent. The guerrilla fighter also needs rapid comprehension and an instantaneous ingenuity in order to be able to change tactics depending on the course of the action.

These faculties of adaptability and inventiveness in popular armies are what ruin the statistics of the warmongers and bring them to a halt.

The guerrilla fighter must never for any reason leave a wounded compañero at the mercy of the enemy troops, because this means abandoning him or her to an almost certain death. At whatever cost, the wounded must be removed from the combat zone to a secure place. The greatest exertions and the greatest risks must be taken in this task. The guerrilla soldier must be an extraordinary compañero.

At the same time they should be close-lipped. Everything that is said and done in their presence should be kept strictly to themselves. A single unnecessary word should never be let slip, even with one's own comrades-in-arms, since the enemy will always try to plant spies among the ranks of the guerrillas in order to discover their plans, location, and livelihood.

Besides the moral qualities mentioned, the guerrilla fighter should possess a range of very important physical qualities. The guerrilla fighter must be indefatigable, able to produce an additional effort even when exhaustion seems unbearable. Profound conviction, evident in every facial expression, forces the guerrilla to take another step, and this not the last one, since it will be followed by another and another and another until the place designated by his chiefs is reached.

The guerrilla should be able to endure extremities, to withstand not only the privations of food, water, clothing, and shelter to which they are frequently subjected, but also the sickness and wounds that often must be cured by nature without much help from the surgeon. This must be so, because **many** times the individual who leaves the guerrilla zone to recover from sickness or wounds will be assassinated by the enemy.

To meet these conditions guerrilla fighters need an iron constitution that will enable them to resist all these adversities without becoming ill, and to use their lives as hunted animals as another way of strengthening themselves. Assisted by a natural adaptability, guerrillas become part of the landscape in which they fight.

All these considerations raise the question: what is the ideal age for a guerrilla fighter? These limits are always very difficult to define precisely, because individual and social characteristics differ. A peasant, for example, will be much more resistant than a person from the city. A city dweller who is accustomed to physical exercise and a healthy life will be much more effective than a person who has spent their life behind a desk. But generally the maximum age of combatants in the totally nomadic stage of the guerrilla struggle should not exceed 40, although there can be exceptional cases, above all among the peasants. One of the heroes of our struggle, Commander Crescencio Pérez, came to the Sierra Maestra when he was 65 and he immediately became one of the most useful members of the troop.[3]

We could also ask if the members of the guerrilla band should be drawn from a certain social class. It has already been stated that the social composition should be adjusted to that of the particular operational zone; in other words, the combatant nucleus of the guerrilla army should be composed of peasants.

---

3.   In green, Che has written: **Check.**

The peasant is evidently the best soldier; but the other strata of the population should by no means be excluded or deprived of the opportunity to fight for a just cause. In this respect there are important individual exceptions.

We have not yet set a lower age limit. We believe that minors less than 16 years old should not be accepted, except in very special circumstances. In general these young kids, virtually children, do not have sufficient development to cope with the tasks, the weather, and the suffering to which they will be subjected.

The best age for a guerrilla fighter varies between 25 and 35 years, a stage at which life has assumed a definite shape for most people. An individual who sets out at that age, abandoning their home, children, and entire world, must have thóught through their responsibility and made a firm decision not to retreat a step. There are extraordinary cases of children who have reached the highest ranks of our Rebel Army as combatants, but this is not common. For every one of them who displayed great fighting qualities, there were dozens who should have been returned to their homes and who frequently became a dangerous burden for the guerrilla band.

As we have said, the guerrilla fighter is a soldier who carries their house on their back like a snail; therefore, one's backpack must be arranged in such a way that the least number of utensils will be of the greatest possible service. Only what is indispensable will be carried, and will be guarded at all times as something fundamental and never to be lost other than in extreme adversity.

By the same token, armaments will be only what can be carried. Reprovisioning is very difficult, especially bullets; to keep them dry, always to keep them clean, to count them one by one so that none is lost — these are the watchwords. And the gun should always be kept clean, well greased, and with the barrel shining. It is advisable for the leader of each group to impose some penalty or punishment on those who do not maintain their arms in these conditions.

People with such outstanding commitment and firmness must have an ideal that sustains them in the adverse conditions we have described. This idea is simple, straightforward, without any great pretension, and in general does not go very far; but it is so firm, so clear, that a person will give their life for it without the least hesitation. For almost all peasants this ideal is the right to have and work a piece of their own land and to enjoy just social treatment. For workers it is to have a job, to receive an adequate wage, as well as just social treatment. For students and professionals more abstract ideas such as liberty might be their motives for the struggle.[4]

This raises the question: what is the life of the guerrilla fighter like? The normal routine is the long hike. Let us take the example of a mountain guerrilla fighter located in wooded regions under constant enemy harassment. In these conditions the guerrilla band moves during daylight hours, without eating, in order to alter its position; when night arrives, camp is set up in a clearing near a water supply according to a routine, each group assembling in order to eat together; at dusk the fires are lighted with whatever is around.

Guerrilla fighters eat when they can and anything they can. Sometimes fabulous meals disappear down combatants' gullets; at other times they fast for two or three days without reducing their capacity for work.

---

4. In red, Che has written: **Expand with the development of the war.**

Home will be the open sky; between it and a hammock a sheet of waterproof nylon is placed, and beneath the sheet and hammock are the guerrilla fighter's treasures: their backpack, gun, and ammunition. There are places where it is not wise to remove one's shoes, because of the possibility of a surprise attack by the enemy. Shoes are another precious treasure. Whoever has a pair has the security of a happy existence within the limits of the prevailing circumstances.

The guerrilla fighter might go for days in a place, avoiding all contact that has not been previously arranged, staying in the roughest zones, familiar with hunger, at times thirst, cold, heat; sweating during the continuous marches, letting the sweat dry on one's body and adding to it new sweat with no possibility of regular cleanliness (although this also depends somewhat on the individual's disposition, as does everything else).[5]

During the recent war, on entering the town of El Uvero* after a 16-kilometer march and a battle that lasted two hours and 45 minutes in a hot sun (after several days spent in very adverse conditions along the sea with **high** temperatures and a boiling sun), our bodies gave off a peculiar and offensive odor that repelled anyone who came near. Our noses were completely accustomed to this lifestyle; guerrilla fighters' hammocks are known for their characteristic, individual odor.

In such circumstances breaking camp should be done rapidly, leaving no traces behind; vigilance must be extreme. For every 10 guerrillas asleep, one or two should be on watch, with the guards changed continually and a sharp vigil maintained over all the entrances to the camp.

---

5.   Che marked the words in brackets for deletion.
*   The story of "The Battle of El Uvero" is told in Che's *Reminiscences of the Cuban Revolutionary War*, Melbourne & New York: Ocean Press, 2006, pages 78–87.

Campaign life teaches several tricks for preparing meals, some to help speed preparation; others to add seasoning with little things found in the forest; still others for inventing new dishes that give a more varied character to the guerrillas' menu, which is mainly roots, grains, salt, a little oil or lard, and very sporadically, pieces of the meat of some animal that has been slaughtered. **This** is the scenario for a group operating in tropical regions.

Within the framework of the combatant's life, the most interesting event — the one that brings convulsions of joy and puts new vigor in everyone's steps — is the battle. As the climax of the guerrilla's life, combat is sought at the opportune moment, either when an enemy camp sufficiently weak to be annihilated has been located and investigated; or when an enemy column is advancing directly toward the territory occupied by the liberating force. The two cases are different.

Against an enemy camp the action will be a thin encirclement and essentially will become a hunt for the members of the columns that try to break the encirclement. An entrenched enemy is never the favorite prey of the guerrilla fighter; he prefers the enemy to be on the move, nervous, not knowing the terrain, fearful of everything and without natural protections for defense. To be behind a parapet with powerful arms for repelling an offensive, however bad the situation, will never be the same as being in a long column that is suddenly attacked in two or three places and cut. If the attackers are not able to encircle the column and destroy it totally, they will withdraw prior to any counterattack.

If there is no possibility of defeating those entrenched in a camp by means of hunger or thirst or by a direct assault, the guerrilla band should retire after the encirclement has yielded its destructive fruits in the relieving columns. In cases where the guerrilla column is too weak and the invading column too strong, the action should be concentrated against the vanguard. There should be a special preference for this tactic, whatever the hoped-for result, since after the leading ranks have been hit several times, thereby spreading the news among the soldiers that those in the front are constantly dying, the reluctance to occupy those positions will provoke nothing less than mutiny. Therefore, attacks should target that point even if they also target other points of the column.

The guerrilla fighters' ability to perform their functions and adapt themselves to the environment will largely depend on their equipment. Even though united in small groups, they will have individual needs. Besides their regular shelter, they should have in their backpack everything needed for survival in case they find themselves alone for some time.

In presenting this list of equipment we refer essentially to what should be carried by an individual in rough country at the beginning of a war, with frequent rainfall, some cold weather, and harassment by the enemy; in other words, in a similar situation to that we faced at the beginning of the Cuban war of liberation.

The equipment of the guerrilla fighter is divided into the essential and the accessory. Among the first is a hammock. This provides adequate rest; it is easy to find two trees from which to hang it; and, in cases where one sleeps on the ground, it can serve as a mattress. Whenever it is raining or the ground is wet, a frequent occurrence in tropical mountain zones, the hammock is indispensable for sleeping. A piece of waterproof nylon cloth complements it. The nylon should be large enough to cover the hammock when tied from its four corners, and with a line strung through the center to the same trees from which the hammock

HAMMOCK WITH A NYLON ROOF

hangs. This last line serves to make the nylon into a kind of tent by raising a center ridge and allowing water to run off.*

It is cold in the mountains at night so a blanket is indispensable. It is also necessary to carry a garment such as a jacket

---

* The illustrations and captions from the original edition are reproduced here, drawn by the combatant Lieutenant Hernando López, who after the revolution remained under Che's command until Che left for the Congo in 1965. Among his designs of great historical value are the banknotes issued by the National Bank of Cuba from 1960 onwards, bearing Che's signature as the bank's president.

that will help one to bear the extreme changes of temperature. Clothing should be rough work trousers and shirt, which may or may not be a uniform. Shoes should be of the best possible **construction** and moreover, since without good shoes marches are very difficult, they should be one of the first articles laid up in reserve.

Since guerrilla fighters carry their homes in their backpacks, the latter is very important. The more primitive types may be made from any kind of sack carried by two ropes; but canvas backpacks found in the market or made by a harness maker are preferable. The guerrilla fighter should always carry some personal food besides that which the troop carries or consumes in its camps. Indispensable articles are: lard or oil, which is necessary for fat consumption; canned goods, which should not be consumed except in circumstances where food for cooking cannot be found or when there are too many cans and their weight impedes the march; preserved fish, which has great nutritional value; condensed milk, which is also nourishing, particularly because of the large quantity of sugar it contains; something for the sweet tooth; powdered milk, which is also easily transportable; sugar is another essential part of the supplies, as is salt, without which life becomes sheer martyrdom; and something with which to season the meals, such as onion, garlic, etc., depending on what can be found locally. This completes the list of the essentials.

The guerrilla fighter should carry a plate, knife, and fork, which will serve all the various necessary functions. The plate can be a camping or military type or a pan that can be used for cooking anything from a piece of meat to *malanga** or a potato, or for brewing tea or coffee.

---

* *Malanga* is a starchy root vegetable native to Cuba and the Caribbean.

Special greases are necessary for maintaining rifles; and these must be carefully administered — sewing machine oil is very good if there is no special oil available. Cloths that can be used for cleaning weapons are needed as well as a rod for cleaning the inside of the gun, something that should be done often. The ammunition belt can be a commercial type or homemade, depending on the circumstances, but it should be constructed so that not a single bullet will be lost. Ammunition is the key to the battle, without which everything else is in vain; it must be guarded like gold.

A canteen or a bottle for water is essential, since it will often be needed where water is not available. Medicines that have a general use should be carried: for example, penicillin or some other type of antibiotic, preferably the types taken orally, well sealed; medicines for lowering fever, such as aspirin; and others to treat the endemic diseases of the area. These may be malaria tablets, sulfas for diarrhea, medicine against all types of parasites; in other words, the medicine should be appropriate for the region. Where there are poisonous animals it is recommended to carry the right serums. Surgical instruments will complete the medical equipment. Small personal items for attending to less important injuries should also be included.

A common and extremely important comfort in the guerrilla fighter's life is a smoke, such as cigars, cigarettes, or pipe tobacco; a smoke is a great friend to the solitary soldier in moments of rest. Pipes are useful, because they mean every last piece of tobacco from the butts of cigars and cigarettes can be used at times of scarcity. Matches are extremely important, not only for lighting a smoke, but also for starting fires; this is one of the great problems in the woods in rainy periods. It is preferable to carry both matches and a lighter, so that if the lighter runs out of fuel, matches can be a substitute.

Soap should be carried, not just for personal hygiene, but also for cleaning eating utensils, because intestinal infections or irritations are frequent and can be caused by spoiled food left on dirty cookware. With this set of equipment, the guerrilla fighter can be assured that he will be able to live in the woods under adverse conditions, no matter how bad, for as long as required to overcome the situation.

There are accessories that are sometimes useful and others that are a bother but are very useful. The compass is one of these; at the start this will be used a lot for orientation, but little by little knowledge of the countryside will make it unnecessary. In mountainous regions a compass is not much use, because impassable obstacles will probably cut off the route indicated. Another useful article is an extra nylon cloth for covering all the equipment when it rains. Remember that in tropical countries it rains continuously during certain months, and that water is the enemy of everything the guerrilla fighter must carry: food, ammunition, medicine, paper, and clothing.

A change of clothing can be carried, but this usually shows inexperience. The usual practice is to carry no more than an extra pair of pants, eliminating underwear and other articles, such as towels. The guerrilla fighter learns through experience to conserve their energy in carrying a backpack from one place to another, and will, little by little, get rid of everything that has no essential value.

Along with a piece of soap that is equally useful for washing utensils as for personal hygiene, a toothbrush and paste should be carried. It is worthwhile also to bring a book, which can be exchanged for others among members of the guerrilla band. These books can be good biographies of past heroes, histories, or economic geographies, preferably of the country, and works of general character that can raise the cultural level of the soldiers and discourage the tendency toward gambling or other undesirable pastimes. There are periods of boredom in the life of the guerrilla fighter.

Whenever there is extra space in the backpack, it should be used for food, except in those zones where food is easily and readily available. Sweets or food of lesser importance that supplement the basic items can be carried. Crackers can be one of these, although they take up a lot of space and break up into crumbs. In thick forests a machete is useful; in very wet places a small bottle of gasoline or some light resinous wood for kindling, such as pine, will make fire building easier when the wood is wet.

A small notebook and pen or pencil for taking notes and for letters to the outside or communication with other guerrilla bands should always be part of the guerrilla fighter's equipment. Pieces of string or rope should be kept as these have many uses, along with needles, thread, and buttons for clothing. The guerrilla fighter who carries this equipment will have a solid house on their back, rather heavy but furnished to ensure a comfortable life during the hardships of the campaign.

3 ORGANIZATION OF A GUERRILLA BAND

There is no rigid scheme for the organization of a guerrilla band; there will be innumerable differences depending on the environment in which it operates. For the sake of argument, we will suppose that our experience has a universal application, but it should always be kept in mind that there will possibly be new forms that better match the particular characteristics of a given armed group.

The size of the component units of the guerrilla force is one of the most difficult problems to deal with: the number and composition of the troops will differ, as we have already explained. Let us suppose a force is situated on favorable terrain, mountainous, with conditions not so bad as to necessitate perpetual flight, but not good enough for establishing a base of operations. The combat units of an armed force in this situation should not be more than 150 guerrillas, and even this number is rather high; ideally, the unit would be about 100. This constitutes a column and would be led by a commander, according to Cuban organizational practice, remembering that in our war we abolished the ranks of corporal and sergeant because of their identification with the dictatorship.*

On this basis, the commander heads this entire force of 100 to 150 guerrillas; and there will be as many captains as there are groups of 30 to 40. The captain's role is to direct and unify their platoon, making it fight almost always as a unit and looking after the distribution of guerrillas and the general organization. In guerrilla warfare, the squad is the functional unit. Each squad, made up of approximately eight to 12 fighters, is commanded by a lieutenant, who leads the group as the captain leads the platoon, but is always subordinate to the captain.

The operational tendency of the guerrilla band to function in small groups makes the squad the true unit. Eight to 10 guerrillas are the maximum that can act as a unit in a battle in these conditions: therefore, the squad, which will often be separated from the captain even though they fight on the same front, will operate under the orders of its lieutenant; there are exceptions, of course. A squad should not be broken up or kept

---

*   Fulgencio Batista first rose to power through the "sergeants' revolt" in
     1933.

dispersed at times when there is no fighting. Each squad and platoon should know who the immediate successor is in case the chief is killed, and such a person should be sufficiently trained to be able to take over their new responsibilities immediately.

One of the fundamental problems of the troop is food supply; in this everyone from the last person to the chief must be treated alike. This acquires great importance, not only because of the chronic shortage of supplies, but also because meals are the only daily events. The troops, who have a keen sense of justice, measure the rations with a sharp eye; the least favoritism toward anyone should never be allowed. If, in certain circumstances, the meal is served to the entire column, a regular order should be established and strictly observed, and at the same time the quantity and quality of food given to each person should be carefully checked. In the distribution of clothing the problem is different, these being articles of individual use. Here there are two considerations: first, the demand for necessities, which will almost always be greater than the supply; and second, the length of service and merits of each of the applicants. The length of service and merits, something very difficult to calculate precisely, should be noted in a special book by someone assigned this responsibility under the direct supervision of the column chief. The same should occur with other articles that become available and are of individual rather than collective use. Tobacco and cigarettes should be distributed according to the general rule of equal treatment for all.

This task of distribution should be a specifically assigned responsibility. It is preferable that the designated persons be attached directly to the command. The command performs, therefore, the very important administrative tasks of liaison, as well as all the other special tasks that are necessary. Officers of the greatest intelligence should be included in the command, and soldiers attached to the command should be the brightest and most dedicated, since they will usually bear a greater burden than the rest of the troop. Nevertheless, they can have no special treatment at mealtime.

Each guerrilla fighter carries their full equipment; there is also a range of implements for general use that should be equitably distributed within the column. For this, too, rules can be established, depending on the number of unarmed persons in the troop. One method is to distribute all extra materiel, such as medicines, medical, dental or surgical instruments, extra food, clothing, general supplies, and heavy weapons equally among all platoons, which will then be responsible for their safekeeping. Each captain will distribute these supplies among the squads, and each chief of squad will distribute them among the guerrillas. Another solution, which can be used when not all the troop is armed, is to create special squads or platoons assigned to transport; this works out well, since it leaves the soldier who already has the weight and responsibility of their rifle free of an extra load. In this way the danger of losing materiel is reduced, since it is concentrated; and at the same time there is an incentive for the porter to carry more and to carry better and to demonstrate more enthusiasm, since this is the way he will win his right to a weapon in the future. These platoons will march in the rear and will have the same duties and the same treatment as the rest of the troop.

The tasks to be performed by a column will vary depending on its activities. While encamped, there will be special teams for keeping watch. These should be experienced, specially trained, and they should receive some special reward for this duty. This might be increased independence, or, if there is an excess of sweets or tobacco after proportional distribution to each column, something extra for the members of those units that carry out special tasks. For example, if there are 100 guerrillas and 115 packets of cigarettes, the 15 extra packs of cigarettes can be distributed among the members of these units. The vanguard and the rearguard units, separated from the rest, will have special vigilance duties; but each platoon should also have its own sentries. The farther from camp the watch is maintained, the greater the security of the group, especially when it is in open country.

The places chosen should be high, overlooking a wide area by day and difficult to approach by night. If the plan is to stay several days, it is worthwhile to construct defenses that will permit sustained fire in case of an attack. These defenses can be demolished when the guerrilla band moves on, or they can be left if circumstances no longer make it necessary to hide the column's tracks.

Where permanent camps are established, the defenses should be constantly improved. Remember that in a mountainous zone on carefully chosen ground, the only heavy weapon that is effective is the mortar. Using roofs reinforced with local materials, such as wood, rocks, etc., it is possible to make good refuges that are difficult for the enemy forces to approach and which will offer protection for the guerrilla forces from mortar shells.

It is very important to maintain discipline in the camp, and this should have an educational function. The guerrilla fighters should be required to go to bed and get up at set times. Games that have no social function and that damage troop morale and the consumption of alcohol should be prohibited. All these tasks are performed by a commission of internal order elected from those combatants with the greatest revolutionary merit. Their other role is to prevent the lighting of fires in places where they might be visible from a distance, or that raise columns of smoke before nightfall; they must also see that the camp is kept tidy and that when the column leaves no traces remain, if this is necessary.

Great care must be taken with fires that can leave traces for a long time; they should be covered over with earth; papers, cans, and scraps of food should also be burned. Total silence must prevail when the column is on the march. Orders are passed by gestures or by whispers passed from mouth to mouth until they reach the last person. If the guerrilla band is marching through unknown places, cutting a road, or being led by a guide, the vanguard will be approximately 100 or 200 meters or even more ahead, depending on the nature of the terrain. Wherever confusion might occur about the route, a guerrilla will be left at each turning to wait for those following, and this will be repeated until the last person in the rearguard has passed. The rearguard will also be somewhat separated from the rest of the column, keeping a watch on the roads in the rear and trying to erase the troop's tracks as far as possible. If there is a side road that might present a danger, it is always necessary to have a group keeping watch on it until the last person has passed. It is more practical that each platoon utilize its own members for this special duty, with each having the obligation to pass the guard to the following platoon and then to rejoin their own unit; this process will be continued until the entire troop has passed.

The march should be uniform and in an established order, always the same. Thus it will always be known that platoon number one is the vanguard, followed by platoon number two, and then platoon number three, which may be the command;

then number four, followed by the rearguard or platoon number five or other platoons that make up the column, always in the same order. During night marches silence should be even stricter and the distance between each combatant shorter, so that no one will get lost and make it necessary to shout or shine any light. Light is the enemy of the guerrilla fighter at night.

If all this marching is directed toward an attack, then on reaching a given point — the place to which everyone will return after the objective is accomplished — the extra weight of such things as backpacks and cooking utensils will be deposited, and each platoon will proceed with nothing more than its arms and fighting equipment. Trustworthy people, who have checked out the terrain and have observed the location of the enemy guards, should have reviewed the point of attack. The leaders, knowing the orientation of the base, the number of men that defend it, etc., will make the final plan for the attack and send combatants to their positions, always keeping in mind that a good number of the troops should be assigned to intercept reinforcements. In cases where the attack against a base is merely a diversion designed to provoke the sending of reinforcements along roads that can be easily ambushed, someone should communicate the result to the command as soon as the attack has been carried out, in order to break the encirclement, if necessary to prevent being attacked from the rear. In any case there must always be a sentry on the roads that lead to the combat area while the encirclement or direct attack is being carried out.

By night a direct attack is always preferable. It is possible to capture a camp if there is enough momentum and the required presence of mind and if the risks are not excessive.

An encirclement necessitates waiting and taking cover, closing in on the enemy steadily, trying to harass him in every way, and above all, trying to force him by fire to come out. When the circle has been closed to short range, the "Molotov cocktail" is a weapon of extraordinary effectiveness. Before coming within range for the "cocktail," shotguns with a special charge can be employed. These weapons, which in our war we christened "M-16s," consist of a 16-caliber sawed-off shotgun with a pair of legs added in such a way that with the butt of the gun they form a tripod. The weapon will thus be mounted at an angle of about 45 degrees; this can be adjusted by moving the legs back and forth. It is loaded with an open shell from which all the shot has been removed. A cylindrical stick extending from the muzzle of the gun is used as the projectile. A bottle of gasoline resting on a rubber base is placed on the end of the stick. This apparatus will fire the burning bottles 100 meters or more with a fairly high degree of accuracy. This is an ideal weapon for encirclements when the enemy has a lot of constructions made of wood or other inflammable material; it is also good for firing against tanks in hilly country.

Once the encirclement ends in victory, or, having achieved its objective, is withdrawn, all platoons retire in an orderly manner to the place where the backpacks were left, and the normal routine is resumed.

In this phase, the guerrilla fighter's nomadic life produces not only a deep sense of fraternity among the guerrillas but at times also dangerous rivalries between groups or platoons. If these are not channeled to create a beneficial spirit of emulation, there is the risk that the unity of the column will be damaged. The education of the guerrilla fighters is crucial from the very beginning of the struggle; the social purpose of the fight and their duties should be explained in order to deepen their understanding, and to give them lessons in morale that will

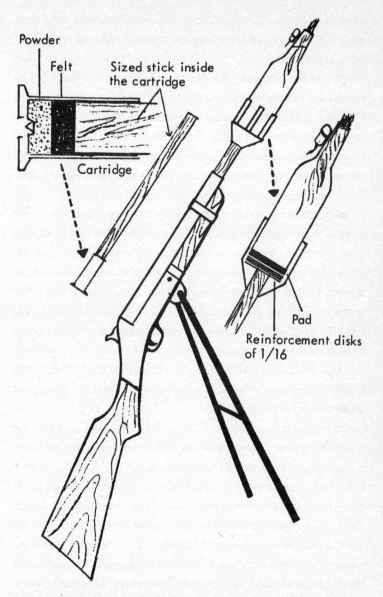

Powder

Felt

Sized stick inside the cartridge

Cartridge

Pad

Reinforcement disks of 1/16

ADAPTATION OF THE "MOLOTOV COCKTAIL" TO A RIFLE

help forge their characters. Each experience should be a new source of strength and not simply one more episode in the fight for survival.

One of the greatest elements of education is example. The chiefs must therefore constantly present an example of a pure and committed life. A soldier's promotion should be based on courage, ability, and a spirit of sacrifice; those who do not possess these qualities to the highest degree should not be given responsible assignments, because this may lead to unfortunate incidents at any time.

The conduct of the guerrilla fighter will be judged whenever he approaches a house to ask for something. The residents will draw favorable or unfavorable conclusions about the guerrilla band depending on the manner in which any service, food, or other necessity is solicited, and the methods used to get what is wanted. The chief should discuss this problem in detail, emphasizing its importance; he should also teach by example. On entering a town, all drinking of alcohol should be prohibited and the troops should be exhorted beforehand to display the best possible discipline. The entrances and exits to the town should be constantly watched.

The organization, combat ability, heroism, and spirit of the guerrilla band will undergo a test of fire during encirclement by the enemy — the most dangerous situation of the war. In our guerrilla jargon in the recent war, the phrase "encirclement face" described the fear evident in someone who was frightened. The hierarchy of the deposed [Batista] regime arrogantly called its campaigns "encirclement and annihilation." Nevertheless, for a guerrilla band that knows the countryside and that is bound ideologically and emotionally to its chief, this is not a particularly serious problem. There is only a need to take cover, to try to slow up the enemy's advance, impede their action with heavy equipment, and wait for nightfall, the guerrilla fighter's natural ally. Then, with the greatest possible stealth, after exploring and choosing the best route, the band will depart, utilizing the most adequate means of escape and maintaining absolute silence. It is extremely difficult in the conditions of darkness to prevent a group of guerrillas from escaping encirclement.

4 COMBAT

Combat is the most important drama in the guerrilla life. It occupies only a short time; but nevertheless these stellar moments acquire an extraordinary importance, since each small encounter is a battle of a fundamental kind for the combatants.

We have already pointed out that an attack should be carried out in such a way as to guarantee victory. Besides general observations regarding the tactical role of attack in guerrilla warfare, the different features of each action should be noted. In the first instance, we will describe the type of battle conducted on favorable terrain, because this is the original model of guerrilla warfare; and it is in this aspect that certain principles must be examined before dealing with other problems through a study of practical experience. Warfare on the plain is always the result of an advance by the guerrilla bands consequent on their being strengthened and on changed conditions; this implies an increase in the guerrillas' experience and their ability to use this experience to their possible advantage.

In the first stage of guerrilla warfare, enemy columns will deeply penetrate insurgent territory; depending on the strength of these columns two different types of guerrilla attacks can be made. In chronological order, the first is to inflict systematic losses on the enemy's offensive capacity over a certain number of months. This action is concentrated on the vanguards; unfavorable terrain restricts the advancing columns' ability to defend their flanks; therefore, there will always be one point of the vanguard that is exposed as it penetrates and offers security to the rest of the column. When there are not sufficient combatants and reserves and the enemy is strong, the guerrillas should always aim for the destruction of this vanguard point. The system is simple; only a certain level of coordination is necessary. At the moment when the vanguard appears at the selected place — the steepest possible — a deadly fire is let loose on them, after a certain number of men have been allowed to penetrate. A small group must stall the rest of the column for some time while arms, munitions, and equipment are being collected. The guerrilla soldier should always remember that their source of arms is the enemy and that, except in special circumstances, they should not engage in any battle that will not lead to the capture of weapons.

When the guerrilla band is strong enough, a complete encirclement of the column can be carried out; or at least this impression should be given. In this case, the guerrilla front line must be sufficiently strong and well covered to resist the enemy's frontal assaults, naturally taking into account both offensive power and combat morale. At the moment when the enemy is detained in some chosen place, the rearguard guerrilla forces attack the enemy's rear. In such a selected place, flanking maneuvers will be difficult; snipers, outnumbered, perhaps by eight or 10 times, will have the entire enemy column within the circle of fire. Whenever there are sufficient forces in these cases, all roads should be protected with ambushes in order to block reinforcements. The encirclement will be closed gradually, particularly at night. Guerrilla fighters know the places where they fight, the invading column does not; guerrilla fighters grow at night, and the enemy sees his fear growing in the darkness.

In this way, without too much difficulty, a column can be totally destroyed; or at least will suffer such losses as to prevent its return to battle and to force it to take some time to regroup.

When the guerrilla band has a small force that aims to halt or slow the advance of the invading column, groups of between two and 10 snipers should spread out around the column at each of the four cardinal points. In this situation an assault can begin, for example, on the right flank; when the enemy focuses their response on that flank and fires that way, shooting begins at that moment from the left flank; at another moment from the rearguard or from the vanguard; and so forth.

With a very small expenditure of ammunition it is possible to hold the enemy in check indefinitely.

The tactics for attacking an enemy convoy or position must be adapted to the conditions of the area selected for the combat. In general, the first attack on an encircled place should be made at night against an advance post, with surprise assured. An attack carried out by skillful commandos can easily liquidate a position, thanks to the advantage of surprise. For a regular encirclement the escape routes can be controlled with a few guerrillas and access roads defended with ambushes; these should be spread out in such a way that if one is unsuccessful, falls back, or simply withdraws, a second remains, and so on successively. In cases where there is no surprise factor, the success of an attempt to overrun a camp will depend on the capacity of the encircling force to block the attempts of the rescue columns. In these cases, artillery, mortars, airplanes, and tanks will usually support the enemy. On favorable terrain, the tank is not so dangerous; it must travel by narrow roads and is an easy victim of mines. The offensive capacity of a formation of these vehicles is generally absent or reduced in these circumstances, since they must proceed in single file or at most two abreast. The best and surest weapon against the tank is the mine; but in a close fight, which may easily take place in steep places, the "Molotov cocktail" has an extraordinary value. We will not yet talk about the bazooka, which for the guerrilla force is a decisive weapon but difficult to acquire, at least in the first stages. A trench with a roof is a defense against the mortar, which is a formidably potent weapon when used against encirclement; but on the other hand, against mobile attackers it loses its effectiveness unless it is used in large batteries. Artillery does not play a big role in this type of fight, since it has to be located where there is suitable access and it does not see the targets, which are constantly shifting. Aviation constitutes the principal arm of the oppressor forces, but its power of attack is also much reduced by the fact that its only targets are small trenches, generally hidden. Aircraft can drop high-explosive or napalm bombs, both of which constitute inconveniences rather than real dangers. Moreover, as the guerrillas draw as close as possible to the enemy's defensive lines, it becomes very difficult for planes to effectively attack the positions of the vanguard.

For attacks against camps made of wood or inflammable constructions the "Molotov cocktail" is a very important arm at a short distance. At longer distances, bottles containing inflammable material with the fuse lighted can be launched from a 16-caliber shotgun, as described earlier.

Of all the different types of mines, the most effective is the remotely exploded mine, although it requires the most technical know-how; but contact, fuse, and above all, electric mines

ANTI-TANK TRAP

with their lengths of cord are also extremely useful, and on mountainous roads constitute defenses for the popular forces that are virtually invulnerable.

A good defense against armored cars traveling along roads is to dig sloping ditches in such a way that the tank enters them easily and afterwards cannot get out, as the picture shows. These can easily be hidden from the enemy, especially at night or when infantry cannot advance in front of the tanks because of resistance by the guerrilla forces.

Another common form of enemy advance in zones that are not too steep is in trucks that are more or less open. Armored vehicles head the columns and the infantry follows behind in trucks. Depending on the strength of the guerrilla band it may be possible to encircle the entire column, following the general rules; or attacking some of the trucks and simultaneously exploding mines can split it. Swift action is necessary in order to seize the arms of the fallen enemy and withdraw.

For an attack on open trucks, a weapon of great importance, which should be used to its full potential, is the shotgun. A 16-caliber shotgun with large shot can sweep 10 meters, nearly the whole area of the truck, killing some of the occupants, wounding others, and provoking an enormous confusion. Grenades, if available, are also excellent weapons for these situations.

For all these attacks, surprise is fundamental because, at least at the moment of firing the first shot, it is one of the basic requirements of guerrilla warfare. Surprise is not possible if the peasants of the zone know the insurgent army is present. For this reason all movements of attack should be made at night. Only guerrillas of proven discretion and loyalty should know about these movements and establish the contacts. The march should be made with backpacks full of food, in order to be able to live two, three, or four days in the ambush areas.

The discretion of the peasants can never really be trusted, first because there is a natural tendency to talk and to discuss events with other family members or with friends; and also because of the enemy soldiers' inevitably cruel treatment of the population after a defeat. Terror can be sown, and this terror leads to someone's talking too much, revealing important information, in the effort to save their life.

In general, the site selected for an ambush should be at least one day's march from the guerrilla band's regular camp, since the enemy will almost always know more or less accurately where it is.

We said before that the nature of fire in a battle indicates the location of the opposing forces: on one side, violent and rapid firing by the soldier of the line, who has plenty of ammunition as a rule; on the other side, the methodical, sporadic fire of the guerrilla fighter who knows the value of every bullet and who endeavors to expend it with the greatest economy, never firing one shot more than necessary. It is not reasonable to allow an enemy to escape or to fail to use an ambush to the full in order to save ammunition, but the amount to be expended in particular circumstances should be calculated in advance and the action carried out according to these calculations.

Ammunition is the big problem for a guerrilla fighter. Arms can always be obtained, and those acquired are not used up by the guerrillas as ammunition is; moreover, arms are generally captured with their ammunition, but ammunition is never or rarely obtained alone. Each confiscated weapon will have its load, but does not contribute to others because there is no extra. The tactical principle of saving firepower is fundamental in this type of warfare.

A guerrilla chief who takes pride in their role takes great care in withdrawal. This should be timely, rapid, and managed in order to save all the wounded and their equipment, the backpacks, ammunition, etc. The rebels should never be surprised while withdrawing, neither should they allow themselves to become surrounded. Therefore, guards must be posted along the selected route at every point where the enemy army is expected to bring forward its troops in an attempt to close a circle; and there must be a communications system that will permit rapid reports when a force tries to surround the rebels.

In combat there must always be some unarmed guerrillas.

These people recover the guns of compañeros who are wounded or dead, guns seized in battle or belonging to prisoners; they will take charge of the prisoners, of evacuating the wounded, and of transmitting messages. There should also be a good corps of messengers with legs of steel and a proven sense of responsibility who will relay the necessary warnings in the least possible time.

The number of people needed in addition to the armed combatants varies; but a general rule is two or three for each 10, including those who will be present at the battle scene and those who will fulfill the necessary tasks in the rearguard, keeping watch on the route of withdrawal and performing the messenger services mentioned above.

When a defensive type of war is being fought, that is to say, when the guerrilla band is attempting to block the passage of an invading column beyond a certain point, the action becomes a war of positions; but at the outset it should always have the element of surprise. In this case, since trenches as well as other defensive systems that will be easily noticed by the peasants will be used, it is necessary that these remain in the friendly zone. In this type of warfare the government generally establishes a blockade of the region, and the peasants who have not fled must go to buy their basic provisions outside the zones of guerrilla action. If these people leave the region at a critical moment, as we are now describing, this can constitute a serious danger because of the information they might pass on to the enemy army. The policy of complete isolation must serve as the strategic principle of the guerrilla army in these circumstances. The defenses and the entire defensive apparatus should be arranged in such a way that the enemy vanguard will always fall into an ambush. It is very important as a psychological factor that the man in the vanguard will die with no chance of escape in every battle, because this creates a growing consciousness of the risk within the enemy army, until eventually no one wants to be in the vanguard; and it is obvious that a column with no vanguard cannot move, since someone has to assume that responsibility. Furthermore, encirclements can be carried out if they are expedient; or diversionary maneuvers such as flank attacks; or the enemy can simply be detained frontally. In every case, places that might be utilized by the enemy for flank attacks should be fortified.

We are now assuming that more guerrillas and arms are available than in the battles described above. Clearly, a large personnel is required to blockade all possible roads leading into a zone, as there might be very many roads. The variety of traps and attacks against armored vehicles will be increased here, in order to give the greatest security possible to the systems of fixed trenches which can be located by the enemy. Generally, in this type of battle, the command will be to defend the positions to the death if necessary; and it is essential to assure every combatant the greatest chance of survival.

The more a trench is hidden from distant view, the better; above all, it is important to provide cover so that mortar fire will be ineffective. Mortars of 60.1 or 85 millimeters, the usual campaign calibers, cannot penetrate a good roof made with simple local materials, such as one made from a base of wood, earth, and rocks covered with some camouflage material. An escape route for an emergency must always be constructed, so that the defender can get away with less risk.

The sketch below shows the way these defenses were constructed in the Sierra Maestra, and the other plan indicates the positions taken in a defensive system of this type.*

---

* In the original edition the mentioned plan does not appear.

REFUGE AGAINST MORTAR FIRE

This outline clearly indicates that fixed lines of fire do not exist. The lines of fire are something more or less theoretical; they are established at certain critical moments, but they are extremely elastic and permeable on both sides. What does exist is a broad "no man's land." But a civilian population inhabits "no man's land" in a guerrilla war, and this civilian population collaborates to some extent with both sides, even though the overwhelming majority supports the insurrectionary band. These people cannot be removed en masse from the zone because of their numbers and because this would create problems of supply for whichever of the contenders tried to provide them with food. This "no man's land" experiences periodic incursions (generally during the daytime) by the repressive forces and at night by the guerrilla forces. This zone becomes a very important maintenance base for the guerrillas and should be nurtured in a political way, always establishing the best possible relations with the peasants and merchants.

In this type of warfare the tasks of **indirect** combatants — in other words, those who do not carry arms — are extremely important. We have already outlined some of the features of contact work in combat zones; but this is an institution within the guerrilla organization. Contacts to the most distant command post or to the most distant guerrilla group should be linked in such a way that messages can be passed along by the most rapid system in the region — whether it is an area easily defended, in other words, favorable terrain, or unfavorable. A guerrilla band operating on unfavorable terrain will be unable to use modern communications systems, such as the telegraph, roads, etc., apart from radios located in military garrisons that can be defended. If these fall into enemy hands, the codes and frequencies must be changed, a rather annoying task.[6]

We are speaking here from memory about experiences in our war of liberation. The daily and accurate report on all the enemy's activities was complemented by our contacts. The espionage system should be carefully studied, well worked

---

6. Che has marked in red from "A guerrilla band operating…" to here, and proposed: **Fix**.

out, and personnel selected with great care. A counter-spy can do enormous damage, but even in less extreme cases, the harm that can result from exaggerated information that misjudges the danger is very great. It is not likely that a risk will be underrated; the tendency of people in the countryside is to overrate and exaggerate. The same mystical mentality that imagines phantasms and all kinds of supernatural beings also creates monstrous armies where there is scarcely a platoon or an enemy patrol. The spy should appear to be as neutral as possible, not known by the enemy to have any connection with the forces of liberation. This is not as difficult a task as it seems; many such individuals are encountered in the course of the war: merchants, professionals, and even clergy can assist in this task and give timely information.

One of the most important features of a guerrilla war is the significant difference between the information that reaches the rebel forces and the information possessed by the enemy. While the latter must operate in regions that are absolutely hostile, encountering sullen silence on the part of the peasants, in nearly every house the rebels have a friend or even a relative, and news is constantly conveyed through the contact system until it reaches the central command of the guerrilla force or of the guerrilla group in the zone.

A serious problem is created when an enemy incursion takes place in territory that has become openly pro-guerrilla, where all the peasants respond to the popular cause. The majority of peasants try to escape with the popular army, abandoning their children and their work; others might even flee with the whole family; some wait to see what will happen. The most serious problem caused by an enemy penetration into guerrilla territory is that of a group of families finding themselves in a tight, possibly desperate situation. They should receive the utmost help, but should also be warned of the consequences of flight into an inhospitable area away from their usual place of work, exposed to the hardships of such an existence.

It is not possible to talk of a "pattern of repression" by the people's enemies. Although the general methods of repression are always the same, they usually commit crimes of greater or lesser intensity depending on specific social, historical, and economic circumstances. There are places where the departure of a person for the guerrilla zone, leaving their family and home, provokes no great reaction. Elsewhere, this is enough to provoke the burning or seizure of their belongings, or even the death of all members of their family. Adequate distribution and organization of the peasants who are going to be affected by an enemy advance must be arranged, depending on the local customs in the war zone or country concerned.

Obviously, preparations must be made to expel the enemy from the territory by taking action against their supplies, completely cutting their lines of communication, destroying their attempts to supply themselves through the actions of small guerrilla bands, and in general forcing them to devote large numbers of men to the problem of supplies.

In all combat situations a very important element is the correct utilization of reserves wherever battle begins. Because of its character, a guerrilla army can rarely count on reserves, since it always strikes so that every individual's efforts are regulated and focused. Nevertheless, some guerrillas should be positioned ready to respond to an unforeseen development, to block a counter-offensive, or to handle a situation at any moment. Within the organization of the guerrilla band, assuming that the conditions and possibilities allow, a utility platoon can be kept ready to be dispatched to the place of greatest danger. It might be christened the "suicide platoon" or something along those lines, a title that truthfully reflects its role. This "suicide platoon" should be everywhere a battle is decided: in the surprise attacks against the vanguard, in the defense of the most vulnerable and dangerous positions, in other words, wherever the enemy threatens to break the steadiness of the line of fire. It should be made up strictly of volunteers. Admittance to this platoon should be regarded **as a** great honor. Over time it becomes the darling within the guerrilla column, and the guerrilla fighter who wears its insignia enjoys the admiration and respect of all their compañeros.

5 BEGINNING, DEVELOPMENT, AND END OF A GUERRILLA WAR

We have now thoroughly defined the nature of guerrilla warfare. Next, we will discuss the ideal development of this war, from the emergence of a single nucleus on favorable terrain and beyond.

In other words, we will theorize further on the basis of the Cuban experience. At the start, there is a more or less armed, more or less homogeneous group that devotes itself almost exclusively to hiding in the roughest and most inaccessible places, making little contact with the peasants. It strikes a lucky blow and its fame grows; a few peasants, dispossessed of their land or engaged in a struggle to preserve it, and young idealistic members of other classes join the nucleus; acquiring greater audacity, it starts to operate in populated areas, making more contact with the local people; it repeats attacks, always fleeing afterwards; suddenly it engages in combat with some column or other and destroys its vanguard. People continue to join; it has increased in number, but its organization remains exactly the same; less cautious, it ventures into more populous zones.

Later it sets up temporary camps for several days; it abandons these on receiving news of an approaching enemy army, after being bombed, or when it becomes aware of such dangers. The numbers in the guerrilla band increase as work among the masses converts every peasant into an enthusiast for the war of liberation. Finally, an inaccessible place is chosen, a settled life begins, and the first small industries are established: a shoe factory, a cigar and cigarette factory, a clothing factory, an arms factory, a bakery, hospitals, possibly a radio transmitter, a printing press, etc.

The guerrilla band now has an organization, a new structure. It is the head of a large movement with all the characteristics of a small government. A court is established for the administration of justice, laws might be promulgated, and the work of indoctrination of the peasant masses continues, now also extended to any local workers, drawing them into the cause. An enemy action is launched and defeated; the number of rifles increases; with these the number of people fighting with the guerrilla band increases. The time arrives when its radius of action will not have increased in the same proportion as its personnel; at that moment a force of appropriate size is separated, a column or a platoon, perhaps, and this moves to another combat zone.

The work of this second group will begin with rather different characteristics because of the experience that it brings and because of the influence of the troops of liberation on the war zone. The original nucleus also continues to grow; it has now received substantial support in food, sometimes in guns, from various places; recruits continue to arrive; the administration of government, with the promulgation of laws, continues; schools are established, permitting the indoctrination and training of recruits. The leaders learn steadily as the war develops, and their ability to command develops with the added responsibilities of the qualitative and quantitative growth of their forces.

If there are remote territories, a group sets out in that direction at a certain moment, in order to confirm the advances that have been made and to continue the cycle.

But there is also an enemy territory, unfavorable for guerrilla warfare. Small groups begin to penetrate there, assaulting the roads, destroying bridges, planting mines, and sowing alarm. With the ups and downs characteristic of warfare the movement continues to grow; by this time the extensive work among the masses makes easy movement of the forces possible in unfavorable territory, and so opens the final stage, which is urban guerrilla warfare.

Sabotage increases significantly throughout the entire zone. Life is paralyzed; the zone is conquered. The guerrillas then move on to other zones, where they confront the enemy army along defined fronts; by now heavy arms have been captured, perhaps even some tanks; the fight is more equal. The enemy falls when a series of partial victories becomes transformed into definitive victories, in other words, when the enemy has to accept battle in conditions imposed by the guerrilla band; there he is annihilated and compelled to surrender.

This is a sketch of what occurred in the different stages of the Cuban war of liberation; but it has a universal significance. Nevertheless, it will not always be possible to count on the same degree of intimacy with the people, the conditions, and the leadership that existed in our war. It is unnecessary to state:

Fidel Castro epitomizes the ultimate qualities of a combatant and statesman; our journey, our struggle, and our triumph we owe to his vision. We cannot say that without him the victory of the people would not have been achieved; but that victory would certainly have cost much more and would have been less complete.

CHAPTER III:
ORGANIZATION OF THE GUERRILLA FRONT

1 SUPPLY

A good supply system is of primary importance to the guerrilla band. A group of guerrillas in contact with the soil must live from the products of this soil and at the same time ensure that the livelihood of those who provide the supplies, the peasants, is maintained. Especially at the beginning of the difficult guerrilla struggle, it is not possible for the group to dedicate its efforts to producing its own food, apart from the fact that these supplies could be easily discovered and destroyed by the enemy in territory likely to be completely penetrated by the repressive forces. In the first stages, therefore, supply is always internal.

As the guerrilla struggle develops, it will be necessary to arrange supply from outside the combat territory. At first, the band survives only on whatever the peasants have; occasionally it might be possible to reach a store to buy something, but it is never possible to have supply lines because there is no territory in which to establish them. The supply line and the food store are conditional on the development of the guerrilla struggle.

The first task is to gain the absolute confidence of the residents of the zone; and this confidence is won by a positive approach to their problems, by help and a constant orientation program, by defending their interests and punishing anyone who attempts to take advantage of the instability in which they live in order to pressure, dispossess the peasants, seize their harvests, etc. The approach should be simultaneously soft and hard: soft and spontaneously helpful to all those who honestly sympathize with the revolutionary movement, hard against anyone attacking it outright, fomenting dissension, or simply passing on important information to the enemy army.

Little by little the territory will be consolidated, and then actions will be easier. The fundamental principle must be always to pay for all merchandise taken from a friend. This might be crops or items from commercial establishments. They will often be donated, but at other times the economic conditions of the peasantry prevent such donations, and there are cases in which necessity forces the guerrilla band to take food from stores without paying for it, simply because there is no money. In this instance, the merchant should always be given a bond, a promissory note, something that acknowledges the debt, "the bonds of hope" discussed previously. It is better to use this method only with people who are outside the liberated territory, and in such cases to pay as soon as possible all or at least part of the debt. When conditions have improved sufficiently to maintain a territory permanently free from the rule of the opposing army, it is possible to establish collective plantings, whereby the peasants work the land for the benefit of the guerrilla army. In this way an adequate, permanent food supply is guaranteed.

If the volunteers for the guerrilla army greatly outnumber its arms, and political circumstances prevent these people from entering zones dominated by the enemy, the rebel army can put them to work directly on the land, harvesting crops; this guarantees supply and adds something to the service record of combatants and their prospects for future promotion. Nevertheless, it is preferable that the peasants sow their own crops, so that this work is performed more efficiently, with more enthusiasm and skill. When conditions have further ripened, depending on the crops involved it is possible to arrange the purchase of entire harvests, which can be left in the field or in a warehouse for the use of the troops.

When mechanisms are established to supply the peasant

population as well, all food supplies can be concentrated in order to facilitate a system of barter among the peasants, with the guerrilla army acting as intermediary.

If conditions continue to improve, taxes can be established; these should be as low as possible, especially for the small producer. It is important to pay attention to every detail of relations between the peasant class and the guerrilla army, which emanates from that class.

Taxes might be collected sometimes in money or in the form of a part of the harvest, which will increase the food supplies. Meat is one of the primary necessities. Its production and preservation must be guaranteed. If the zone is not secure, peasants with no apparent connection to the guerrillas can establish farms that can produce chickens, eggs, goats, and pigs, starting with stock that has been bought or confiscated from the large landowners. In the areas with big estates there are usually large numbers of cattle. These can be killed and salted and the meat maintained in condition for consumption for a long period of time.

This can also be a source of hides. A more or less primitive leather industry can be developed to provide leather for shoes, one of the fundamental accessories in the struggle. In general, essential foods are the following (depending on the zone): meat, salt, vegetables, starches, or grains. The basic food is always produced by the peasants; it might be *malanga* as it was in the mountainous regions of Oriente province in Cuba; it might be corn, as in the mountainous regions of Mexico, Central America, and Peru; potatoes, in Peru; in other zones, such as Argentina, beef; wheat in others; but it is always necessary to guarantee a basic food supply for the troops as well as some kind of fat to assist in food preparation; these might be animal or vegetable fats.

Salt is one of the essential supplies. When close to the sea and able to get to it, small dryers should be established immediately; these will guarantee some production in order to always have a reserve and the ability to supply the troops. Remember that in rough places such as these, where only some of the foods are produced, it is easy for the enemy to establish an encirclement that can greatly damage the flow of supplies into the zone. It is better to plan for such eventualities through peasant groups and civil organizations in general. The residents of the zone should have a minimum food supply on hand that will permit them at least to survive, even though poorly, during the hardest phases of the struggle. An attempt should be made to collect rapidly a good provision of foods that do not decompose — grains, corn, wheat, rice, etc., which can last quite a long time; also flour, salt, sugar, and all types of canned goods; furthermore, the essential seeds should be sown.

The time will arrive when all the food problems of the troops in the zone are solved, but large quantities of other items will be needed: leather for shoes, if it has not been possible to create an industry for supplying the zone; cloth and all the additional things necessary for clothing; paper, a press or mimeograph machine for newspapers, ink, and various other implements. In other words, the need for products from the outside world will increase as the guerrilla bands become more organized and the organization becomes more complex. In order to meet these needs adequately the organized supply lines must function perfectly. These organizations are composed basically of friendly peasants; they should have two poles, one in the guerrilla zone and one in a city. Departing and radiating out from the guerrilla zones, supply lines will spread throughout the whole territory, permitting the passage of materials. Little by little the peasants become accustomed to the danger (in small groups they can work marvels) and come to deposit whatever is required in the indicated spot without running extreme risks. These errands can be run at night with mules or other similar transport animals or with trucks, depending on the area. In this way, a very good supply can be achieved. This type of supply line is for areas near the operational zone.

It is also necessary to organize a supply line to remote areas, which should provide the money needed for making purchases and also the implements that cannot be produced in small towns or provincial cities. The organization will be assisted with direct donations from sectors sympathetic to the struggle, exchanged for secret "bonds," which should be delivered. The personnel charged with the management of this operation should always be strictly controlled. Serious consequences should follow any neglect of the indispensable moral duties involved in this responsibility. Purchases can be made with cash and also with "bonds of hope" when the guerrilla army, having departed from its base of operations, threatens a new zone. In these circumstances, there is no way to avoid seizing merchandise from its owner, who will have to rely on the good faith and capacity of the guerrillas to pay their debts.

For all supply lines that pass through the countryside, it is necessary to have a series of houses, terminals, or way-stations, where supplies can be hidden during the day while waiting to be moved by night. Only those directly in charge of the food supplies should know these houses. The least possible number of local residents should know about this transport operation, and these must be individuals in whom the organization has the greatest confidence.

The mule is one of the most useful animals for these tasks.

With an incredible resistance to fatigue and an ability to walk in the steepest zones, the mule can carry more than 100 kilograms for days. Requiring only simple food, mules are an ideal means of transport. The mule train should be properly provided for with horseshoes, and the muleteers should understand their animals and take great care of them. In this way it is possible to have regular four-footed armies of unbelievable effectiveness. But often, despite the strength of the animal and its ability to bear up through the hardest days, difficulty of passage will make it necessary to leave the cargo in particular spots. To avoid this necessity, a special team should be assigned to cut trails for this kind of animal. If all these conditions are met, if an adequate organization is created, and if the rebel army maintains the required excellent relationship with the peasants, an effective and lasting supply for the entire troop is guaranteed.

2 CIVIL ORGANIZATION

The civil organization of the insurrectional movement is very important on both the external and the internal fronts. Naturally, their features are as different as their functions, although they both perform tasks that fall under the same name. The collections that can be carried out on the external front, for example, are not the same as those that can take place on the internal front; the same goes for the tasks of propaganda and supply. Let us begin with the tasks on the internal front.

On considering the "internal front," we are referring to a territory largely dominated by the forces of liberation. Further, it is assumed that the zone is suitable for guerrilla warfare, because when the right conditions do not exist, in other words, when the guerrilla struggle is taking place in unsuitable terrain, the guerrillas can extend their reach but not deepen it; they can create channels through new areas, but cannot establish an internal mechanism because the entire zone is penetrated by the enemy. On the internal front we might have a range of organizations that perform specific roles to improve administrative efficiency. Generally, propaganda belongs directly to the guerrilla army, but it also can be separated if kept under its control. (This matter is so important that we will discuss it elsewhere.) Collections are a function of the civil organization, as are the general tasks of organizing the peasants and also the workers, if they are present. Both these should be run by one council.

Collections, as we explained in the previous chapter, can be conducted in various ways: through direct or indirect taxes, through direct or indirect donations, and through confiscations; all this goes to complete the large part of the guerrilla army's supplies.

Bear in mind that the zone should never be impoverished by the direct actions of the rebel army, even though it will be indirectly responsible for the impoverishment that results from enemy encirclement, a fact that the adversary's propaganda will repeatedly point out. Precisely for this reason, conflicts should not be created by direct causes. For example, there should be no regulations that prevent the farmers in a liberated zone from selling their produce outside that territory, except in extreme and transitory circumstances and with a full explanation of these exceptions to the peasantry. Every act of the guerrilla army should always be accompanied by propaganda explaining the reasons for it. These reasons will generally be well understood by peasants who have sons, fathers, brothers, or relations within this army, which has become their own.

Considering the importance of relations with the peasantry, organizations should be created to make regulations for them, organizations that exist not only within the liberated zone, but also have connections with the adjacent areas. Precisely through these connections it is possible to penetrate a zone for a future expansion of the guerrilla front. The peasants will sow the seed with oral and written propaganda, with accounts of life in the other zone, of the laws that have already been issued to protect the small peasant, of the spirit of sacrifice of the rebel army; in a word, they create the necessary atmosphere for helping the rebel troops.

The peasant organizations should also have connections of some kind that will permit the transport and sale of crops by the rebel army networks in enemy territory through more or less benevolent intermediaries, more or less friendly to the peasant class. The merchant can be devoted to a cause for which he might take risks, but he is also devoted to money and this means he will take advantage of any opportunity to gain a profit.

We have already mentioned the importance of the department of road construction in connection to supply problems. When the guerrilla band has attained a certain level of development, it might have four or five more or less permanent centers, and will no longer wander about through various regions without a camp. Routes should be established ranging from small trails allowing the passage of a mule to good roads for trucks. In all this, the capacity of the rebel army's organization must be kept in mind, as well as the offensive capacity of the enemy, who might destroy these constructions and even make use of roads built by their opponent to reach the camps more easily. The essential rule is that roads are for assisting supply in places where no other solution is possible; they should not be constructed except in circumstances where there is virtual certainty that the position can be maintained against an adversary's attack.

Another exception would be roads built without great risk to facilitate communication between points that are not of vital importance.

Furthermore, other means of communication can be established. One of these that is extremely important is the telephone, the lines of which can be strung in the forest conveniently using trees for posts. There is the advantage that they are not visible to the enemy from above. The telephone also presupposes a zone that the enemy cannot penetrate.

The council — or central department of justice, revolutionary laws, and administration — is one of the vital features of a guerrilla army fully constituted and with its own territory. The council should be directed by an individual who knows the laws of the country; all the better if he or she understands the necessities of the zone from a juridical point of view; he or she can proceed to draft a series of decrees and regulations that help the peasants normalize and institutionalize life in the rebel zone.

For example, during our experience in the Cuban war we issued a penal code, a civil code, rules for supplying the people, and guidelines for the agrarian reform. Subsequently, the laws were passed setting qualifications for candidates in the national elections that were to be held later; the Agrarian Reform Law of the Sierra Maestra was also established. The council is likewise in charge of accounting operations for the guerrilla column or columns; it is responsible for handling financial problems and at times intervenes directly in issues of supply.

All these recommendations are flexible, based on an experience in a particular place, conditional on its geography and history; they will be modified in different geographical, historical, and social situations.

Besides the council, the general health of the zone must be considered; this might involve central military hospitals that can provide the most complete care to all the peasants. Whether adequate medical treatment can be given will depend on the stage reached by the revolution. Civil hospitals and civil health administration, where officers and army personnel have the dual function of caring for the people and showing them how to improve their health, are linked directly to the guerrilla army. The major health problems among people in these conditions are rooted in their total ignorance of elementary principles of hygiene and this aggravates their already precarious situation.

The collection of taxes, as mentioned above, is also a function of the general council.

Warehouses are very important. As soon as a place is taken that can serve as a base for the guerrilla band, warehouses should be established in the most orderly fashion possible. These will guarantee minimal care of goods and, most importantly, will provide the control needed for equalizing distribution and keeping it equitable in the future.

On the external front, the functions are different both in terms of quantity and quality. For example, propaganda should provide a national orientation, explaining the victories won by the guerrillas, calling on workers and peasants to take effective mass action, and providing news of any victories on its own front. Soliciting funds is completely secret and should be carried out with the greatest possible care, isolating small collectors in the chain completely from the treasurer of the organization.

This organization should be spread throughout areas that complement one another so as to form a whole: zones that might be provinces, states, cities, villages, depending on the size of the movement. In each organization there must be a finance commission that takes charge of the disposal of funds collected. Money can be collected by selling bonds or through direct donations. When the struggle is more advanced, taxes can be collected; when industries come to recognize the great force that the insurrectional army possesses, they will agree to pay. Procurement of supplies should be adjusted to the needs of the guerrilla bands; a supply chain is organized so that the more common items are procured nearby, and things that are scarce or impossible to find locally are sought in larger centers. An effort should be made to keep the chain as limited as possible, known to the smallest number of people; in that way it can carry out its mission for a longer time.

Sabotage should be directed by the civil organization in the external sector, in coordination with the central command. In special circumstances, after careful analysis, assaults on individuals will be initiated. In general, we do not consider this desirable, except for the purpose of eliminating some figure notorious for his villainies against the people and the virulence of his repression. Our experience in the Cuban struggle shows that it would have been possible to save the lives of many fine comrades who were sacrificed in the performance of missions of little value. Sometimes these can result in the reprisal of enemy bullets and a loss of combatants that does not match the results obtained. Indiscriminate assaults and terrorism should not be employed. Much more preferable is an effort directed at large concentrations of people in whom the revolutionary idea can be planted and nurtured, so that at a critical moment they can be mobilized and, with the help of the force of arms, tip the balance in the revolution's favor.

This also requires the popular organizations of workers, professionals, and peasants, who work at sowing the seed of the revolution among their respective masses, explaining issues, providing revolutionary publications for reading, teaching the truth. Truth must be one of the features of revolutionary propaganda. In this way, the masses will slowly be won over. Those who do the best work can be selected for incorporation into the rebel army or assigned to other big responsibilities.

This is the outline of civil organization within and outside the guerrillas' territory during a popular struggle. There are possibilities of improving all these features significantly; I repeat again, I am discussing here our experience in Cuba; new experiences can vary and improve these concepts. We offer an outline, not a bible.

3 THE ROLE OF WOMEN

The part women can play in the development of a revolutionary process is of extraordinary importance. This needs to be stressed because in all our countries, with their colonial mentality, there is a certain underestimation of women that becomes real discrimination.

Women are capable of performing the most difficult tasks, of fighting beside men; and despite current belief, do not create conflicts of a sexual nature among the troops **if a sufficient ideological and organizational base exists.**[1]

In the rigors of a combatant's life a woman is a compañero who brings the qualities appropriate to her sex, but she can work the same as a man and she can fight; she is weaker, but no less resistant than a man. She can perform every combat task that a man can at a given moment, and on certain occasions in the Cuban struggle she performed a relief role.

---

1. Added in red in the original.

Naturally, female combatants are a minority. When the internal front is being consolidated, as many combatants as possible who do not possess indispensable physical characteristics should be removed; women then can be assigned a considerable number of specific occupations, of which one of the most important — perhaps the most important — is communication between different combatant forces, especially between those in enemy territory. The transport of things, messages, or money, small items and those of great importance, should be assigned to women in whom the guerrilla army has total confidence; women can act as couriers using a thousand tricks; it is a fact that however brutal the repression, however thorough the search, a woman receives less harsh treatment than a man and can carry her message or an important or confidential object to its destination.

As a simple messenger, either by word of mouth or in writing, a woman can always perform her task with more freedom than a man, attracting less attention and at the same time inspiring less fear of danger in the enemy soldier; a man who commits brutalities will often act on the impulse of fear or apprehension that he himself will be attacked, since this is one form of action in guerrilla warfare.

Women can wear special belts beneath their skirts to carry messages between separated forces, messages to outside the lines, even to outside the country, and also objects of considerable size, such as bullets. In this phase, women can also perform their traditional role in peacetime: a soldier living in the extremely harsh conditions of guerrilla warfare is happy to be able to look forward to a seasoned meal which actually tastes like something. (One of the great tortures of the war was eating a cold, sticky, tasteless mess.) A female cook can greatly improve the diet and, moreover, is easier to assign to these domestic tasks; one of the problems in guerrilla bands is that those who perform it scorn all labor of a civilian character; they are constantly trying to get out of these tasks in order to participate in the active combat forces.

A task of great importance for women is to teach the basics of reading, including revolutionary theory, primarily to the peasants of the zone, but also to the revolutionary soldiers. The organization of schools, which is a part of the civil organization, should be done principally through women, who arouse more enthusiasm among children and enjoy more affection from the school community. Similarly, when the fronts have been consolidated and a rear exists, the role of social worker also falls to women who investigate the various economic and social evils of the zone with a view to changing them as far as possible.

A woman plays an important part in medical matters as nurse, and even as doctor, with an infinitely superior gentleness to that of her rough compañero-in-arms, a gentleness that is so much appreciated at times when a man is helpless, without comfort, perhaps suffering severe pain and exposed to the many kinds of risks that are part of a war of this nature.

Once the stage of creating small war industries has begun, women can also contribute, especially in the manufacture of uniforms, a traditional employment of women in Latin American countries. With a simple sewing machine and a few patterns she can work miracles. Women can take part in all levels of civil organization; they can replace men perfectly well and should do, even to carry weapons if there is a shortage of couriers, although this is a rare occurrence in guerrilla life.

Men and women should be properly educated, in order to avoid all kinds of misconduct that can damage troop morale;

but unattached individuals who love each other should be allowed to marry and live as man and wife in the mountains, in compliance with the simple requirements of the guerrilla band.

4 HEALTH

One of the serious problems a guerrilla fighter confronts is exposure to the accidents of life, especially to wounds and illness, which are very common in guerrilla warfare. The doctor performs an extraordinarily important role in the guerrilla band, not just in saving lives, where their scientific intervention might have little impact because of the limited resources available; the doctor also reinforces the patient morally and makes him or her feel that there is someone nearby who is dedicating all their efforts to minimizing their pain; the doctor gives the sick or wounded the comfort of knowing that someone will remain at their side until they are cured or out of danger.

The organization of hospitals depends largely on the stage of development of the guerrilla band. Three fundamental types of hospital organization corresponding to various stages can be mentioned.

In the first, nomadic phase, the doctor — if there is one — always travels with their compañeros, as just one more person; he or she will probably have to perform all the other functions of the guerrilla fighter, including that of fighting, and will suffer at times the depressing and desperate task of treating patients when the means of saving lives are not available. This is the stage in which the doctor has the most influence over the troops, the greatest impact on their morale. During this period of the guerrilla band's development the doctor achieves their full potential as a true priest, who seems to carry in their poorly equipped backpack the consolation needed by the guerrillas. The value of a simple aspirin to someone who is suffering badly is beyond calculation, when administered by the friendly hand of someone who makes that suffering his own. Therefore, in the first stage, the doctor must be a person who totally identifies with the ideas of the revolution, because their words will affect the troops much more deeply than those of any other member.

In the normal course of events in guerrilla warfare a further stage is reached that might be called "semi-nomadic." There will be camps, occasionally visited by the guerrilla troops; friendly, secure houses where it is possible to store objects and even leave the wounded; and a growing tendency for the guerrilla troop to become settled. At this stage, the task of the doctor is less frustrating; he or she might have emergency surgical equipment in their backpack and another more complete kit for less urgent operations in a friendly house. It will be possible to leave the sick and wounded in the care of peasants who will offer their help with great dedication. The doctor can also count on a greater number of medicines kept in convenient places; as far as possible, these should be completely catalogued, depending on the circumstances. In this same semi-nomadic state, if the guerrilla band operates in places that are absolutely inaccessible, hospitals can be established to which the sick and wounded can go to recover.

In the third stage, when there are zones invulnerable to the enemy, a true hospital network can be constructed. In its most developed form, this might consist of three different types of center. In the combat category there should be a doctor, the combatant most loved by the troops, a fighter, who does not need very extensive knowledge. I say this because their task is principally one of giving relief and preparing the sick or wounded, while the real medical work is performed in hospitals situated more securely. A good surgeon should not be sacrificed in the line of fire.

When soldiers fall in the front line, stretcher-bearers — if available, which will depend on the level of organization of the guerrilla band — will carry the wounded to the first post; if they are not available, the compañeros thémselves will perform this duty. Transport of the wounded in rough zones is one of the most delicate of all tasks and one of the most painful experiences in a soldier's life. The transport of the wounded is probably harder on the compañeros than the wounded soldier, however grave the injury, because of the guerrillas' spirit of sacrifice. The transport can be carried out in different ways depending on the nature of the terrain. In rough and wooded places, which are typical in this kind of warfare, it is necessary to walk in single file. Here the best system is to use a long pole, with the patient carried in a hammock that hangs from it.

The guerrillas take turns carrying the weight, one in front and one behind. They should swap positions with two other compañeros frequently, since the shoulders suffer severely and the individual is gradually worn out carrying this delicate and heavy burden.

After having been checked at the first hospital, the wounded soldier then proceeds with the information of this initial treatment to a second center, where there might be surgeons and specialists, depending on the possibilities of the guerrilla troop, and where more serious life-saving operations are performed and individuals can be relieved from danger — this is the second stage. At a third level, there are much better hospitals that can conduct investigations into causes and effects of illnesses that prevail among the residents of the zone. These hospitals, which correspond to a sedentary life, are not only centers for convalescence and for less urgent operations, but also serve the civil population, where the hygiene specialists have an educational role. Dispensaries that can monitor individual treatment should also be established. If the supply capability of the civil organization is sufficient, the hospitals of this third group can have a range of facilities that provide diagnosis, possibly even laboratory and x-ray facilities.

Other useful individuals are the doctor's assistants. They are generally youths with some vocation and some knowledge, with fairly strong physiques; they do not bear arms, sometimes because their vocation is medicine, but usually because there are insufficient arms for everyone who wants them. These assistants will be in charge of carrying most of the medicines, an extra stretcher, or a hammock, if circumstances make this possible. They must take charge of the wounded in any battle that is fought.

The essential medicines should be obtained through contacts with health organizations that exist in the enemy's territory. Sometimes they can be obtained from such organizations as the International Red Cross, but this should not be counted on, especially in the initial period of the struggle. It is necessary to organize an apparatus that will ensure the rapid transport of the medicines required in case of danger and that will gradually provide all the hospitals with the supplies necessary for their work, military as well as civil. Moreover, contacts should be made in the surrounding areas with doctors who would be able to help the wounded whose cases are beyond the capacities or the facilities of the guerrilla band.

The doctors required for this type of warfare have different characteristics. The combatant doctor, the compañero of the guerrillas, is needed in the first stage; their functions develop as the action of the guerrilla band becomes more complicated and a range of connected organizations is created. General surgeons are the best acquisition for an army of this type. If an anesthetist is available, so much the better; although almost all operations are performed not with gas anesthesia but using largactil and sodium pentothal, which are much easier to administer and easier to procure and preserve. Besides general surgeons, bone specialists are very useful, because fractures often occur from accidents in the zone; they are also often the result of bullet wounds in limbs. The clinic primarily serves the peasant masses, since sicknesses in the guerrilla armies are generally easy for anyone to diagnose. The most difficult task is to cure problems caused by nutritional deficiencies.

In a more advanced stage, if there are good hospitals, there might even be laboratory technicians, in order to have complete facilities. Appeals should be made to all sectors of the profession whose services are needed; it is quite likely that many will respond to this call and come to offer their help. All kinds of medical professionals are needed; surgeons are very useful, so are dentists. Dentists should be advised to come with simple field instruments and a campaign-type drill, with which they can do practically everything necessary.

5 SABOTAGE

Sabotage is one of the invaluable weapons of a people fighting a guerrilla war. Its organization falls under the civil or clandestine branch, since naturally sabotage should only be carried out outside the territories dominated by the revolutionary army; but this organization should be directly commanded and oriented by the guerrillas' general staff, which will be responsible for deciding the industries, communications, or other objectives that are to be attacked.

Sabotage has nothing to do with terrorism; terrorism and personal assaults are entirely different tactics. We sincerely believe that terrorism is negative, that in no way does it produce the desired effects, that it can turn people against a particular revolutionary movement, and that it brings a loss of life to its agents far greater than any benefit. On the other hand, attempts on the lives of particular individuals are acceptable, but only in very special circumstances, where it will eliminate a key opponent. But specially trained, heroic, self-sacrificing human beings should never be used to eliminate a minor assassin whose death might provoke a reprisal and the annihilation of all the revolutionaries involved in the action, and others besides.

Sabotage can be of two types: sabotage on a national scale against particular targets, and local sabotage against combat lines. Sabotage on a national scale should be aimed principally at destroying communications. Each type of communication can be destroyed in a different way; all of them are vulnerable. For example, telegraph and telephone poles are easily destroyed by sawing them almost all the way through, so that at night they appear to be in normal condition, until a sudden kick brings one pole down and this drags along with it all those that are weak, producing a major power failure.

Bridges can be attacked with dynamite; if there is no dynamite, steel bridges can be destroyed very easily with an oxyacetylene blowtorch. A steel truss bridge should be cut in its main beam and in the upper beam from which the bridge hangs. When these two beams have been cut at one end with the torch, they are then cut at the opposite end. The bridge will fall completely on one side and will be twisted and destroyed. This is the most effective way to bring down a steel bridge without dynamite. Railroads can also be destroyed, as can roads and culverts; sometimes trains can be blown up, if the guerrilla band is strong enough.

At certain times, utilizing the right equipment will also destroy the vital industries of each region. In these cases, an overview of the problem is necessary to ensure that a workplace is not destroyed unless such action will be decisive, since the consequences will be massive unemployment and hunger. The enterprises belonging to the potentates of the regime should be eliminated (and attempts made to convince the workers of the need for doing so), unless this will bring very grave social consequences.

We stress the key factor of sabotage against communications. The great strength of the enemy army against the rebels in the less mountainous zones is rapid communication; we must, therefore, constantly undermine that strength by knocking out railroad bridges, culverts, electric lights, telephones; also aqueducts, and in general everything that is necessary for a normal and modern life.

Around the combat lines sabotage should be performed in the same way but with much more audacity, with much more dedication and frequency. Here it is possible to rely on the invaluable assistance of the flying patrols of the guerrilla army, which can descend into these zones and help the members of the civil organization perform the task. Again, sabotage should be aimed principally at communications, but with greater persistence. All factories, all centers of production that are capable of providing the enemy with something necessary to maintain their offensive against the popular forces, should also to be liquidated.

Emphasis should be placed on seizing merchandise, cutting off supplies as far as possible, if necessary intimidating the large landowners who want to sell their farm produce, burning vehicles that travel along the roads, and using them as blockades. It is advantageous in every act of sabotage that frequent contact be made with the enemy army at points not too far away, always following the hit and run tactic. It is not necessary to put up a serious resistance, but simply to show the adversary that in the area where the sabotage has been carried out there are guerrilla forces ready to fight. This forces him to take a large number of troops, to move cautiously, or not to move at all.

In this way, little by little, all the cities in the zone surrounding guerrilla operations will be paralyzed.

6 WAR INDUSTRY

War industries within the guerrilla army sector are the product of a rather long evolution; they also depend on the guerrillas' control of geographically favorable territory. From the time that liberated zones are created and the enemy establishes a strict blockade over all supply chains, different departments can be organized as necessary, as already described. There are two fundamental industries, of which one is the manufacture of shoes and leather goods. It is not possible for a troop to walk without shoes in steep, wooded zones, with rocks and thorns. It is very difficult to march without shoes in such conditions; only the locals, and not all of them, can do it. The rest must have shoes. The industry is divided into two parts, one for putting on half-soles and repairing damaged shoes; the other will be dedicated to the manufacture of rough shoes; there should be a small but complete toolkit for making shoes; because this is a simple industry practiced by many people in such regions it is very easy to create. Connected with the shoe workshop there should always be a workshop making all kinds of canvas and leather goods for the troop's use, such as cartridge belts and backpacks. Although these items are not essential, they contribute to comfort and give a feeling of autonomy, of adequate supply, and of self-reliance to the troop.

An armory is the other vital industry for the small internal organization of the guerrilla band. This also has different functions: the simple repair of damaged weapons, rifles, and other available arms; the manufacture of certain types of combat arms that the inventiveness of the people will create; and the preparation of mines with various devices. When conditions permit, equipment for the manufacture of powder can be added. If it is possible to manufacture the explosives as well as the detonation devices in the liberated territory, brilliant achievements can be made in this area, which is very important because communications **over land**[2] can be completely paralyzed by the appropriate utilization of mines.

Another important group of industries makes iron and tin products. All the blacksmith's labor will be focused on making equipment for the mules, such as shoes. The tinsmith will fabricate plates and canteens, which are especially important. A foundry can be combined with the tinsmith's shop. By melting soft metals it is possible to make grenades, which with a special type of charge will contribute in an important way to the armament of the troop. There should be a technical team

---

2. Che used red to change this word.

for general repair and construction work of various kinds, the "service battery," as it is called in regular armies. With the guerrillas it would operate in the same way, taking care of all necessities, but with nothing of the bureaucratic spirit.

A person must be in charge of communications. They will have as their responsibility not only propaganda communications, such as radio directed toward the outside, but also telephones and all kinds of routes. They will use the civil organization as necessary in order to perform their duties effectively. Remember that we might be in a war in which we are subject to attack by the enemy and that often many lives depend on rapid communication.

For the troop's pleasure, it is a good idea to have cigarette and cigar factories; the tobacco can be bought in selected places and transported to the liberated territory where the items to be consumed by the soldiers can be manufactured. An industry for preparing leather from hides is also of great importance. All these are simple enterprises that can operate quite well anywhere, and are easy to establish in the guerrilla situation. The industry for making leather requires a small cement construction; also it uses large amounts of salt; but it will be an enormous advantage to the shoe industry to have its own supply of material. Salt should be made in revolutionary territory and collected in large quantities. It is made by evaporating water of a high saline content. The sea is the best source, though there might be others. It need not be purified of other ingredients for the purpose of consumption, although it might have a nasty taste at first.

Meat should be preserved in the form of beef jerky, which is easy to prepare. This can save many lives among the troop in extreme situations. It can be preserved with salt in large barrels for a fairly long time, and it can then be used anywhere.

7 PROPAGANDA

The ideas of the revolution should be disseminated through whatever media is available, as broadly as possible. This requires full equipment and an organization, which will consist of two complementary wings covering the entire national area: one for propaganda originating outside the liberated territory, that is, from the national civil organization; and the other for propaganda originating within, that is, from the base of the guerrilla army. In order to coordinate these two forms of propaganda, the functions of which are strictly interlinked, there should be a single director.

Propaganda of the national type from civil organizations outside the liberated territory should be disseminated through newspapers, bulletins, and proclamations. The most important newspapers will be devoted to national affairs in general and will give the public exact information about the state of the guerrilla forces, always observing the fundamental principle that in the long run truth is the best policy. Apart from these publications of general interest, there must be others, more specialized, for different sectors of the population. A publication for the countryside should bring to the peasantry a message from their compañeros in all the free zones who have already felt the beneficial effects of the revolution; this strengthens their aspirations. A workers' newspaper will have similar features, with the sole difference that it cannot always offer a message from the combatant sector of that class, since it is likely that workers' organizations will not operate within the framework of guerrilla warfare until the final stages.

The great watchwords of the revolutionary movement, the watchwords of a general strike (which at an opportune moment will assist the rebel forces) and the need for unity should be explained. Other periodicals can be published; for example, one explaining the tasks of those sectors throughout the entire island that are not combatants but which nevertheless carry out various acts of sabotage, attacks, etc. Within the organization there can be periodicals directed at the enemy's soldiers; these will explain facts of which they are otherwise kept ignorant. News bulletins and movement proclamations are very useful.

The most effective propaganda is that prepared within the guerrilla zone. Priority will be given to the dissemination of ideas among the local people of the zone, explaining the theoretical significance of the insurrection, already understood by them as fact. In this zone there will also be peasant periodicals, the general organ of all the guerrilla forces, and bulletins and proclamations; and besides all these, the radio.

All problems should be discussed by radio — for example, the way to defend oneself from air attacks, and the location of the enemy forces, even citing familiar names among them. National propaganda will use newspapers similar to those prepared outside the liberated territory, but it can include more up to date and more precise news, reporting facts and battles that are extremely interesting to the reader. Information on international affairs will be confined almost exclusively to commentaries on facts that are directly related to the liberation struggle.

The spoken word on the radio, above all, is the most effective propaganda, which can be most easily spread over the entire national area and can appeal to the reason and the sentiments of the people. The radio is a factor of extraordinary importance. At times when war fever is more or less palpitating in every person in a region or a country, the inspiring, burning word enhances this fever and imparts it to all future combatants. It explains, teaches, inflames, and confirms the future positions of both friends and enemies. Nevertheless, the radio should be ruled by the fundamental principle of popular propaganda, which is the truth; it is preferable to tell the truth, however insignificant, than a large lie, artfully embellished. The radio should give reports, especially of battles, of all kinds of encounters, and assassinations committed by the repression; it should also give doctrinal orientations and practical lessons to the civil population; and, from time to time, speeches by the revolutionary leaders.

We consider it useful that the main newspaper of the movement bears a name recalling a great and unifying image, perhaps a national hero or something similar; in-depth articles should also explain where the movement is headed and create a consciousness about the great national problems, besides offering sections of more lively interest to the reader.

8 INTELLIGENCE

"Know yourself and your adversary and you will be able to fight a hundred battles without a single disaster." This Chinese proverb is as valuable for guerrilla warfare as a biblical psalm. Nothing helps the combatant forces more than correct intelligence. This comes spontaneously from the local residents, who will tell their friendly army, their allies, what is happening in various places; but in addition, this should be completely systematized. As we have seen, there should be a postal organization with the right contacts both within and outside guerrilla zones for carrying messages and goods. An intelligence service should also be in direct contact with enemy fronts, which men and women, especially women, should infiltrate; they should be in permanent contact with soldiers and gradually discover what there is to be discovered. The system must be coordinated in such a way that crossing the enemy lines into the guerrilla camp can be achieved without mishap.

If this is done well by competent agents the insurgent camp will be able to sleep more peacefully.

The essential **aspect**[3] of this intelligence will be concerned, as already stated, with the front line of fire or the forward enemy camps that border the no man's land; but it should also develop along with the guerrilla band, increasing its depth of operation and its potential to predict larger troop movements in the enemy's rear. All local people are intelligence agents for the guerrilla band in the places where it is dominant or makes incursions, but it is a good idea to have persons especially assigned to this task. The peasants, not accustomed to precise military language, have a strong tendency to exaggerate, so their reports must be checked. As the spontaneous forms of popular collaboration are established and organized, it is possible to use the intelligence apparatus not only as an extremely important backup but also as a weapon of attack by using its personnel, for example, as "sowers of fear." Pretending to be on the side of the enemy soldiers, they sow fear and instability by spreading discouraging news. Mobility, the basic tactic, can be developed to the maximum. By knowing exactly the places where the enemy troops are going to attack, it is easy to avoid them, or when the time is ripe, to attack them where they least expect it.

---

3. Che used red for this correction.

9 TRAINING AND INDOCTRINATION

The liberation soldier is trained essentially through life in the guerrilla band, and no leader can exist without having learned their difficult role in daily armed exercises. Some compañeros can be taught how to handle arms, concepts of orientation, the correct approach to the civil population, methods of fighting, etc.; but precious time of the guerrilla band should not be consumed in methodical teaching. This only begins when there is a large liberated area and a large number of persons are needed to perform a combat role. Schools for recruits will then be established.

These schools then have a very important function; they will train new soldiers from those who have not passed through that excellent sieve of formidable privations — the life of a guerrilla combatant. From the beginning, other privations must be suffered to convert them into the truly chosen. After having passed through very difficult tests, they will be able to be incorporated into the kingdom of a beggar army that moves without leaving a single trace. They should have two types of physical exercises: gymnastics as part of commando training, which demands agility in attack and withdrawal; and hard and exhausting hikes that will toughen the recruit for this kind of existence. Above all, they should live in the open air. They should suffer all inclemency of the weather in close contact with nature, as the guerrilla band does.

The school for recruits must have workers who will take care of its supply needs; for this there should be cattle sheds, grain sheds, gardens, a dairy, everything necessary, so that the school will not be a burden on the general finances of the guerrilla army. The students can rotate the tasks of supply, either as punishment for bad conduct or simply as volunteers.

TARGET PRACTICE

This will depend on the nature of the zone where the school is being held. We believe that a good principle is to assign volunteers and to cover the remaining work quotas with those who have the poorest conduct and show the poorest disposition for learning warfare.

The school should have a small medical facility with a doctor or nurse, depending on possibilities; this will give the recruits the best possible attention.

Shooting is the basic training. The guerrilla fighter should be properly trained in this respect, so he or she will try to use the least possible amount of ammunition. Practice begins with what is called dry shooting. This consists of placing the rifle firmly on a kind of wooden apparatus as shown in the picture. Without moving or firing the rifle, the recruits point at a **movable board with a hole in the center**, until they think they have the center exactly in their sight. **The board allows** each "shot" to be marked on the fixed board behind, which remains stationary. If the mark for **several** tries gives a single point, this is excellent. When circumstances allow, practice with 22-caliber rifles can start; this is very useful. If there is an excess of ammunition or an urgent need for preparing soldiers, they will have the chance to use bullets.[4]

One of the most important courses in the school for recruits, one considered basic and which can be given anywhere in the world, is what to do in an air attack. Our school had been positively identified from the air and was attacked once or twice a day. The way in which the students responded to this continuous bombardment on their regular place of instruction showed which of the young guerrillas had the potential to be useful soldiers in battle.

The important aspect in such a school for recruits — something that must never be neglected — is indoctrination; this is crucial because individuals **enter** without a clear conception of why they have come, with only a few vague concepts of liberty, freedom of the press, etc., without any **great ideological foundation.** Because of this, indoctrination should be carried out with the greatest dedication and for as long as possible. These courses should **teach** the basic history of the country, **explained** with a clear grasp of the economic factors behind each historical event; the classes should include accounts of the national heroes and their response to certain injustices; and finally an analysis of the national situation or the situation in the zone. A short primer should be studied thoroughly by all members of the rebel army, as it might become a draft for future use in popular education.

There should also be a teacher training school, where texts to

---

4. For all corrections on this page, Che used red.

be used can be selected, considering the contribution that each book can make to the educational process.

Reading should be encouraged at all times, with an effort to promote books that are worthwhile and that develop the recruit's ability to encounter the world of letters and great national questions. The desire for further reading will follow; their circumstances will awaken a new aspiration for understanding in the soldiers; little by little, the recruits will observe in their routine tasks the enormous advantages of those who have passed through the school over the rest of the troop, their capacity for analyzing problems and their superior discipline, which is another of the fundamental things that the school must teach.

This discipline that is internal, not mechanical, and based on a rational understanding, can produce formidable results in moments of combat.

10 THE ORGANIZATIONAL STRUCTURE OF THE ARMY OF A REVOLUTIONARY MOVEMENT

As we have seen, a revolutionary guerrilla army, whatever its zone of operations, must rely on a noncombatant organization for a range of extremely important auxiliary missions. Later, we will see that this whole organization converges to lend the army the utmost help, since the armed struggle is obviously the key factor in the triumph.

The military organization is headed by a commander, in the Cuban case by a commander-in-chief, who names the leaders of the different regions or zones; these leaders have authority to govern their respective territories of activity, to name column commanders — the chiefs of each column — and the other lower officers.

Under the commander-in-chief there will be the zone commanders; under them several columns of varying size, each with a column commander; under the column commanders there will be captains and lieutenants, which, in our guerrilla organization, was the lowest grade. In other words, the lieutenant was the first rank above a soldier.

This is not a model but a description of one case, of how the organization worked in one country where it proved possible to triumph over an army that was fairly well organized and well armed. In other respects, too, our experience is not a model. It simply shows how, as events unfold, it is possible to organize an armed force. The ranks certainly have no importance, but what is important is that no rank should be conferred that does not correspond to the effective battle force commanded; no one should be promoted who has not passed through the sieve of sacrifice and struggle, for that would conflict with morality and justice.

This description applies to a well-developed army, already capable of waging serious combat. In the first stage of the guerrilla band, the chief can take whatever rank he likes, but he will still command only a small group.

One of the most important features of military organization is disciplinary punishment. Discipline must be one of the bases of action of the guerrilla force (this must be stressed again and again), which, as we have also said, should emanate from a carefully reasoned internal conviction; this produces an individual with inner discipline. When discipline is violated, the offender must be punished, whatever their rank, and punished severely, in a way that hurts.

This is important, because a guerrilla soldier feels pain differently from a soldier in a regular army. The punishment of spending 10 days in jail is a magnificent period of rest for the guerrilla fighter: 10 days with nothing to do but eat, no marching, no work, no standing the customary guards, sleeping at will, resting, reading, etc. From this it is obvious that the deprivation of liberty is not recommended for a guerrilla situation.

Where the combat morale of the individual is very high and self-respect strong, deprivation of their right to be armed can constitute a real punishment and provoke a positive reaction. In such cases, this is an effective punishment.

The following painful incident is an example. During the battle for one of the cities in Las Villas province in the final days of the war, we found an individual asleep in a chair while others were attacking positions in the town center. When questioned, the man responded that he was sleeping because he had been deprived of his weapon for firing accidentally; he was told that this was not the way to react to punishment and that he should regain his weapon, not in this way, but in the front line of combat.

A few days went by, and as the final assault on the city of Santa Clara began, we visited the first-aid hospital. A dying man there extended his hand, recalling the episode I described, stating that he had been able to recover his weapon and had earned the right to carry it. He died a short time afterwards.*

This was the level of revolutionary morale that our troops attained through the continual exercise of armed struggle. It is not possible to achieve this at the beginning, when many

---

* This incident is recounted in "The Final Offensive and the Battle of Santa Clara," in *Reminiscences of the Cuban Revolutionary War*, op. cit., page 260.

are still frightened and subjective tendencies put a brake on revolutionary influences; but it is reached eventually through work and through the force of continual example.

Long night watches and forced marches can also serve as punishments; but such marches are not really practical, as they exhaust the individual for no reason other than that of punishment, and they require guards who also wear themselves out; the guards suffer the further inconvenience of having to keep a watch on the persons being punished, who are soldiers of limited revolutionary mentality.

In the forces directly under my command I imposed the punishment of arrest with privation of sweets and cigarettes for slight offenses and a total deprivation of food for worse offenses. The result was magnificent, even though the punishment was terrible; it is recommended only in very special circumstances.[5]

---

5. At the bottom of the page, in red, Che wrote the note: **It is necessary to expand on the real problems of structure.**

CHAPTER IV: APPENDICES

1 UNDERGROUND ORGANIZATION OF THE FIRST GUERRILLA BAND

Guerrilla warfare **develops in accordance with a series of laws,**[1] some derived from the general laws of warfare and others related to its special characteristics; if it is really intended to begin the struggle from some foreign country or from different and remote regions within the country, it is obvious that underground work must start with a small nucleus of initiates, acting apart from the mass action of the people. If the guerrilla movement arises spontaneously from the reaction of a group of individuals to some form of coercion, it is possible that the organization of this guerrilla nucleus to defend itself from annihilation will be enough. Nevertheless, in general, guerrilla warfare starts from a well-considered act of will: a chief with some prestige starts an uprising for the salvation of his people, beginning this work in difficult conditions in a foreign country.

Almost all popular movements against dictators in recent times have suffered from the same fundamental weakness of inadequate preparation; the rules of conspiracy, which demand extreme secrecy and caution, have not generally been observed. The governmental power of the country often knows about the intentions of the group or groups in advance, either through its secret services or from imprudent revelations, or in some cases, from outright declarations, as occurred in our case, for example, when the invasion was announced and encapsulated in Fidel Castro's phrase: "In the year 1956 we will be free or we will be martyrs."

---

1. Red was used for this correction.

Absolute secrecy, a total denial of information to the enemy, should be the primary base of the movement; secondly — and also very important — is the selection of the human material. At times this selection can be made easily, but at other times it will be extremely difficult because it is necessary to rely on those elements that are available, long-time exiles or persons who offer themselves when the call goes out simply because they understand that it is their duty to enroll in the battle to liberate their country, etc. There might not be the appropriate facilities for thoroughly checking these individuals. Nevertheless, even though elements of the enemy regime might be able to infiltrate the movement, it is inexcusable that they might later be able to pass on information; in the period just prior to an action all participants should be concentrated in secret places known only to one or two individuals, they should be under the strict vigilance of their chiefs and without the slightest contact with the outside world. Whenever there are concentrations, whether in preparation for departure or in order to carry out preliminary training or simply to hide from the police, it is always necessary to keep all new personnel, about whom there is no clear knowledge available, away from the key places.

In underground conditions no one, absolutely no one, should know anything more than what is strictly indispensable; and there should not be any talk in front of **those who do not need to know something**.[2] When certain concentrations are formed, it is necessary even to control letters that leave and arrive in order to have total knowledge of the contacts that the individuals maintain; no one should be permitted to live alone, or to go out alone; personal contacts of the future member of the liberating

---

2. Red was used for this correction.

army, contacts of any type, should be prevented by every means. However positive the role of women in the struggle, it must be emphasized that they can also play a destructive part. The temptation women present to young men living away from their usual lifestyle in a special psychological situation is well known. As dictators are well aware of this weakness, they will try to use it for infiltrating spies. Occasionally, the relationship of these women with their superiors is clear and even notorious; at other times, it is extremely difficult to prove even the slightest evidence of contact; therefore, it is necessary also to prohibit relations with women.

The revolutionary in a clandestine situation preparing for war should be a complete ascetic; this is also a test of one of the qualities that will later be the basis of their authority: discipline. If an individual repeatedly disobeys the orders of his superiors and makes contact with women, develops friendships that are not permitted, etc., he should be separated immediately, not merely because of the potential danger in the contacts, but simply because of the violation of revolutionary discipline.

Unconditional help should not be expected from a government, whether friendly or simply negligent, that allows its territory to be used as a base of operations; the situation should always be regarded as though the movement was operating in a totally hostile environment. The few exceptions to this only confirm the general rule.

We cannot speak here of the number of persons that should be trained. This depends on so many and such varied conditions that it is practically impossible to specify; it is only possible to discuss the minimum number with which a guerrilla war might be initiated. In my opinion, considering the inevitable desertions and limitations, in spite of the rigorous process of selection, there should be a nucleus of 30 to 50 guerrillas; this figure is sufficient to initiate an armed struggle in any country of the Americas within a favorable territory for operations, where there is hunger for land, persistent injustice, etc.

As already stated, weapons should be the same as those used by the enemy. Always considering that every government is in principle hostile to a guerrilla action being undertaken from its territory, the bands that prepare themselves should not be greater than approximately 50 to 100 guerrillas per unit. In other words, although there is no objection to 500 guerrillas initiating a war, all 500 should not be concentrated in one place. Firstly, because so many will attract attention and in the case of a betrayal or raid, the whole group is destroyed; secondly, it is much more difficult to raid several places at once.

The central headquarters for meetings might be more or less known, and the exiles will go there for all kinds of meetings; but the leaders should be present only occasionally, and there should be no compromising documents. The leaders should use as many different houses as possible, those least likely to be under surveillance. Arms deposits should be distributed in several places, if possible; these locations should be an absolute secret, known to only one or two people.

Weapons should be handed to those who are going to use them only when the war is about to be initiated; this is to avoid punitive action against trainees that might lead to their imprisonment and the loss of arms that are very difficult to procure, when the popular forces are in no state to suffer such a loss.

Another important factor requiring attention is the preparation of the forces for the extremely hard fight that is coming; these forces should have strict discipline, high morale, and a clear comprehension of the task to be performed, without bravado, without illusions, without false hopes of an easy triumph. The struggle will be bitter and long, setbacks will be suffered, almost to the brink of annihilation; only high morale, discipline, faith in final victory, and exceptional leadership can save the situation. This was our experience in Cuba, even though at one time just 12 men formed the nucleus of the future army, because all these conditions were met and because the person who led us was named Fidel Castro.

Besides ideological and moral preparation, thorough physical training is necessary. The guerrillas will, of course, select a mountainous or very rough zone for their operations; at any rate, in whatever situation they find themselves, the basic tactic of the guerrilla army is the march, and neither slow nor tired men can be tolerated. Adequate training therefore includes exhausting hikes day and night, day after day, gradually increasing, always carried on to the brink of exhaustion, using emulation to increase speed. Resistance and speed will be the key to the first guerrilla nucleus; also, a range of theoretical principles should be taught, such as orienteering, reading, and forms of sabotage. If possible, there should be training with military rifles, frequent firing, especially at distant targets, and a lot of instruction about ways to economize bullets.

To the guerrilla fighter, economy and utilization of ammunition down to the last bullet should almost become a religious tenet. If all these warnings are followed, the guerrilla forces can attain their **final** destiny.[3]

---

3. Red was used for this correction.

2 HOLDING POWER

Naturally, ultimate victory cannot be won until the army that sustained the former regime has been systematically and totally destroyed. Furthermore, all the institutions that protected the former regime should be smashed; but as this is solely a guerrilla manual we will limit ourselves to considering the problem of national defense in the case of a war or aggression against the new power.

The first thing we will encounter is world public opinion; "the serious press," the "truthful" news agencies belonging to the monopolies of the United States and other countries will begin an attack on the liberated country, an attack as aggressive and systematic as the laws of popular reform. For this reason not a single element from the former army can be retained. Militarism, blind obedience, traditional concepts of military duty, discipline and morale cannot be eradicated with one blow. Neither can the victors — who are good fighters, decent and kind-hearted, but at the same time generally lacking education — coexist with the vanquished, who are proud of their specialized military knowledge in combat weaponry, mathematics, fortifications, logistics, etc., and who totally despise the uncultured guerrilla fighters.

Of course, there are cases of individual military men who break with the past and join the new organization with a spirit of absolute cooperation. These people are doubly useful, because they combine their love of the people's cause with the knowledge necessary for creating the new popular army. As a consequence of smashing the old army and dismembering it as an institution, and the occupation of its former posts by the new army, it will be necessary to reorganize the new force. Its former guerrilla character, operating to a certain extent under separate chiefs, without any kind of plan, must be restructured; it is very important to emphasize that the operational concepts of the guerrilla band should still serve as the guidelines. In other words, these concepts will determine the organic formation and the best framework for the popular army. Care should be taken to avoid the error we made during the first months of trying to fit the new popular army into the old vestments of military discipline and organization. This error can lead to serious disorder and can lead to a complete lack of organization. **The transition must be made with caution.**[4]

Preparation should begin immediately for the new defensive war that will have to be fought by the people's army, which has been accustomed to independence of command within the common struggle and initiative in the management of each armed group. This army will have two immediate problems: one will be the incorporation of thousands of last-minute revolutionaries, good and bad, whom it is necessary to train in the rigors of guerrilla life and who must be provided with revolutionary indoctrination in accelerated and intensive courses. Revolutionary education, providing the essential ideological unity to the popular army, is the basis of national security both in the long and short runs. The other problem is the difficulty of adaptation to the new organizational structure.

A group should immediately be created to take charge of disseminating the new revolutionary truths among all units of the army. It should explain to the soldiers, peasants, and workers, who have all come from the people, the justice and the truth of each revolutionary act, the goals of the revolution, why

---

4. This addition was made in red, with the note: **Expand**.

there is a struggle, why so many compañeros have died without being able to see the victory. Combined with this intensive indoctrination, accelerated courses of primary instruction that begin to overcome illiteracy should also be organized, in order to raise the level of the rebel army gradually so that it becomes an instrument of high technical qualifications, solid ideological structure, and magnificent combative power.

Time will bring these three qualities. The military apparatus will continue to be perfected over time; the former combatants can be given special courses to prepare them as professional military men who will then give annual courses of instruction to the people joining voluntarily or through conscription. This process will depend on national characteristics and cannot be presented as a model.

From this point on, we are expressing the opinion of the command of [Cuba's] Rebel Army in regard to the policy followed in the concrete situation of Cuba, considering the threat of foreign invasion, the situation in the modern world at the end of 1959 and the beginning of 1960, with the enemy in our sights, analyzed, evaluated, and awaited without fear. In other words, we are no longer theorizing for the instruction of others about what has already been done; rather we are analyzing what others have done in order to apply it ourselves in our own national defense.

As our problem is to theorize about the Cuban case, to locate and test our hypothesis on the map of American realities, we present the following as an epilogue:

3 EPILOGUE: ANALYSIS OF THE SITUATION IN CUBA, PRESENT AND FUTURE[5]

It is now one year since the dictator fled, the culmination of a long civil and armed struggle by the Cuban people. The government's achievements in the social, economic, and political fields are enormous; nevertheless, they should be analyzed, and every conclusion reviewed in order to demonstrate to the people the precise dimensions of our Cuban revolution. This national revolution, fundamentally agrarian in nature, having the enthusiastic support of workers, the middle class, and today even the owners of industry, has acquired a continental and international transcendence, protected as it is by the unshakable determination of the people and by the peculiar features that animate it.

This will not try to summarize, however briefly, all the laws passed, all of them of undeniable benefit to the people. It should suffice to focus on a few of these laws in order to demonstrate the logical course of development, from beginning to end, in the progressive and necessary order that responds to the interests of the Cuban people.

The first alarm bell for the parasitic classes of the country sounds with the rent law, the reduction of electricity rates, and the intervention* in the telephone company and the subsequent reduction in call charges — all decreed in rapid succession.

Those who saw Fidel Castro and those who made this revolution as nothing more than old-style politicians, easily

---

5. This section in the original edition was not numbered and followed directly from the previous section.
*   The term "intervention" refers to the revolutionary government's nationalization of an enterprise.

manipulated idiots with beards as their only distinction, now began to suspect that something more profound was emerging from the bosom of the Cuban people and that their privileges were about to disappear. The word "communism" began to surround the leading figures and the triumphant guerrilla fighters; consequently, the word "anticommunism," the dialectical opposite, attracted all those resentful or dispossessed of their unjust sinecures.

The law on vacant plots and the law on time payments accentuated this sense of malaise among usurious capitalists. But these were minor skirmishes with the reactionaries; everything was still all right and possible. "This crazy kid," Fidel Castro, could be counseled and set on the right path, the good "democratic" path, by a Dubois or a Porter. One had to have faith in the future.

The Agrarian Reform Law came as a tremendous jolt; most of those affected by it now saw clearly. Gaston Baquero, the voice of reaction, was one of the first; he had accurately predicted what would happen and had retired to the more tranquil waters of the Spanish dictatorship. There were still some who believed that "the law is the law," and that other governments had previously promulgated similar laws, theoretically designed to help the people; but carrying out these laws was something else. This unruly and complicated child nicknamed INRA* was regarded at first with peevish and touching paternalism from the ivory towers of learning, pervaded as they were by social doctrines and respectable theories of public finance that were considered beyond the uncultured and absurd mentality of a guerrilla fighter. But INRA advanced like a tractor or a war

---

* INRA: National Institute of Agrarian Reform

tank, because it is both a tractor and tank, breaking down the walls of the great estates as it passed, and creating new social relations in land ownership. This Cuban agrarian reform arose with several important characteristics for the Americas. Yes, it was anti-feudal in the sense that it eliminated the Cuban-style latifundia, annulled all contracts that demanded payment of land rent in crops, and liquidated the servitude existing mainly in coffee and tobacco production, among our most important agricultural products. But it also was an agrarian reform in a capitalist framework to destroy the monopoly pressure that limits the possibilities of human beings, isolated or as collectives; our reform helped peasants work their land honorably and produce without fear of the creditor or the master. From the beginning, it was exemplified by offering the peasants and agricultural workers — those who give themselves to the soil — what they needed in terms of technical assistance from competent personnel; machinery; financial help provided through credits from INRA or para-state banks; and significant help from the "Association of People's Stores" that has been developed on a large scale in Oriente [province] and is in the process of being developed in other provinces. The state stores, replacing the old usurers, provide fair financing and pay a fair price for crops.

In contrast to the three other great agrarian reforms in America (Mexico, Guatemala, and Bolivia) the most important unique feature of the Cuban reform has been the decision to go all the way, without concessions or exceptions of any kind. This thorough-going agrarian reform respects no rights other than the rights of the people, with no discrimination based on class or nationality: the weight of the law falls equally on the United Fruit Company and on the King Ranch, as on the big Creole *latifundistas*.

Under these conditions land is prepared for the production of crops that the country needs — rice, oil-producing grains, and cotton — which are being developed intensively. But the nation is not satisfied and is going to recover all its stolen wealth. Its rich sub-soil, which has been a battlefield of monopolist voracity and struggle, is effectively recovered through the petroleum law. This law, like the agrarian reform and all the measures taken by the revolution, meets Cuba's undeniable needs, responding to the urgent demands of a people that wishes to be free, that wishes to be master of its economy, that wishes to prosper and to reach ever higher goals of social development. But for this very reason it represents an example for the continent that the oil monopolies fear. It is not that Cuba directly hurts the petroleum monopoly substantially; there is no reason to believe the country to be rich in reserves of the precious fuel, even though there are reasonable hopes of obtaining a supply that will satisfy our domestic needs. But Cuba's law provides a palpable example to the brother peoples of America, many of them ravaged by these monopolies or pushed into internal wars in order to satisfy the needs or appetites of competing trusts, while Cuba, on the other hand, shows what is possible in the Americas, and the exact moment when action should be considered. The great monopolies also turn their uneasy gaze on Cuba; not only has the little Caribbean island dared to eliminate the interests of the omnipotent United Fruit Company (the legacy of Mr. Foster Dulles to his heirs), but the empires of Mr. Rockefeller and the Deutsch group have also suffered under the lash of intervention by the popular Cuban revolution.

This law, like the mining law, is the response of the people to those who try to hold them back with threats of force, with air attacks, with all kinds of punishment. Some say that the mining law is as important as the agrarian reform. In general, we do not consider this is so important for the country's economy, but it introduces another new feature: a 25 percent tax on exported products, to be paid by companies that sell our minerals abroad (so that they now leave behind them something other than a hole in the ground). This not only contributes to Cuba's well-being, but also increases the relative strength of the Canadian monopolies in their struggle with the current exploiters of our nickel. Thus the Cuban revolution eliminates the latifundia, limits the profits of the foreign monopolies, limits the profits of the foreign intermediaries that dedicate their parasitic capital to the commerce of importation — launching into the world a new policy in the Americas, which dares to break the mining giants' monopoly, and leaves at least one of them in difficulty. This represents a potent new call to the neighbors of one of the great monopolistic nations, and has repercussions throughout the continent. The Cuban revolution breaks through the barriers of the news media and spreads its truth like a shower of dust among the American masses anxious for a better life. Cuba is the symbol of new nationhood and Fidel Castro the symbol of liberation.

By a simple law of gravity the little island of 114,000 square kilometers and six-and-a-half million inhabitants assumes the leadership of the anticolonial struggle in America, where the serious wavering by other countries has allowed Cuba to take the heroic, glorious, and dangerous advanced post. The economically stronger nations of colonial America, those in which national capitalism develops stunted by the continuous, relentless, and at times violent struggle with the foreign mon-opolies, now cede their place gradually to this small, new champion of liberty, since their governments do not have sufficient force to carry the fight forward. This is not a simple task, nor is it free from danger and difficulties, but requires the backing of an entire people and an enormous charge of idealism and spirit of sacrifice, especially in the virtual isolation we face in the Americas. Small countries have tried to maintain this post before Guatemala: the Guatemala of the quetzal, that dies when imprisoned in a cage, the Guatemala of the Indian Tecum Uman, felled by the direct aggression of the colonialists. Bolivia, the country of Murillo, the proto-martyr of American independence, yielded to the terrible hardships of the struggle after providing three examples that served as the foundation of the Cuban revolution: the suppression of the army, agrarian reform, and nationalization of mines — the greatest source of wealth, and at the same time, the greatest source of tragedy.

Cuba is aware of these previous examples, knows the failures and the difficulties, but also knows that we are at the dawning of a new era in the world; the pillars of colonialism have been swept aside by the force of the national and popular struggle in Asia and Africa. Now the unity of the peoples is not based on religion, customs, desires, racial identification or discrimination, it comes from similar economic and social conditions and from a similar yearning for progress and recovery. Asia and Africa joined hands in Bandung*; Asia and Africa have come to join hands with colonial and indigenous America through Cuba, here in Havana.

On the other hand, the great colonial powers have lost ground in the face of the struggle of the peoples. Belgium and Holland are two caricatures of empires; Germany and Italy have

---

* In 1955, the first meeting was held in Bandung, Indonesia, of the movement that later became the Nonaligned Nations Movement.

lost their colonies. France is bitterly fighting a war that is lost.*
England, diplomatic and skillful, undermines political power
while maintaining the economic connections.

North American capitalism replaced some of the old colonial
capitalisms in the countries that began their independent life,
but it knows that this is transitory and that there is no real
security for its financial speculations in these new territories;
the octopus cannot attach its suckers firmly there. The claws
of the imperial eagle are trimmed. Colonialism has died or is
dying a natural death in all these places.

America is something else. The English lion with its voracious
appetite departed from our America some time ago, when the
charming, young Yankee capitalists installed the "democratic"
version of the English clubs, imposing their sovereign authority
over every one of the 20 republics.

This is the colonial realm of North American monopoly, its
reason for being and its last chance, its own "backyard." If all
the Latin American peoples should raise the flag of dignity, as
Cuba has done, monopoly would tremble; it would have to
accommodate itself to a new political-economic situation and
to a substantial pruning of its profits. Monopoly does not like
profits to be pruned, and the Cuban example, this "bad example"
of national and international dignity, is gaining strength in the
countries of America. Every time an impudent people cries out
for liberation, Cuba is blamed; and Cuba is guilty in the sense
that Cuba has shown the way, the way of a popular armed
struggle against supposedly invincible armies, how to fight in
rough places and wear down and destroy the enemy away from
his bases, in a word, the way of dignity.

---

* A reference to the Algerian war of independence.

This Cuban example is bad, a very bad example, and monopoly cannot sleep peacefully while this bad example remains at its feet, confronting danger, advancing toward the future. It must be destroyed, they declare. Intervene against this bastion of "communism," cry the servants of monopoly disguised as representatives in Congress. "The Cuban situation is very disturbing," say the artful defenders of the trusts. We all know what they mean: "It must be destroyed."

So, what are the options for aggressive action to destroy the bad example? One could be described as purely economic. This starts with a restriction on credit by North American banks and suppliers to all businessmen, national banks, and even the National Bank of Cuba. North American credit is thus restricted, and through the medium of associates an attempt is made to have the same policy adopted in all Western European countries; but this alone is not sufficient.

The denial of credits strikes a first, hard blow at the economy, but recovery is rapid and the balance of trade evens out, since the victimized country is accustomed to living day to day. More pressure is required. The sugar quota becomes part of the dance: yes, no, no, yes. Frantically the calculating machines of the agents of monopoly tally up all their accounts and reach the final conclusion: it is very dangerous to reduce the Cuban quota and impossible to cancel it. Why very dangerous? Because besides being bad politics, it would stimulate the appetite of 10 or 15 other supplier countries, causing them tremendous unease as they would all consider they had a right to more. It is impossible to cancel the quota, because Cuba is the largest, most efficient, and cheapest provider of sugar to the United States, and because 60 percent of the interests that profit directly from the production and commerce in sugar are US interests. Moreover, the balance of trade is favorable to the United States; whoever does not sell cannot buy; and it would set a bad example to break a treaty. Besides, the supposed North American gift of paying nearly three cents above the market price is only the result of North American incapacity to produce sugar cheaply. The high wages and the low productivity of the soil prevent the Great Power from producing sugar at Cuban prices; and by paying this higher price for a product, they are able to impose onerous treaties on all beneficiaries, not only Cuba. It is impossible to eliminate the Cuban quota.[6]

We do not consider it likely that monopolists will employ a variant of the economic approach in bombing and burning cane fields, hoping to cause a sugar shortage. This appears instead to be a measure calculated to undermine confidence in the revolutionary government's authority. (The corpse of the North American mercenary stains more than a Cuban house with blood; it also stains a policy.* And what can be said of the gigantic explosion of arms destined for the Rebel Army?**)

Another vulnerable place where the Cuban economy can be pressured is the supply of raw materials, such as cotton. However, it is well known that there is an over-production of cotton in the world, and any difficulty of this nature would be transitory. Fuel? This requires some attention; it is possible to paralyze a country by depriving it of fuel, and Cuba produces

---

6. The margin of this entire paragraph was marked in green with the observation: **Explain about bagasse** [the residue left after the liquid is extracted from sugarcane].

* In February 1960, a plane that was damaged by its own bomb dropped over Cuban territory crashed, killing the pilot, who was later revealed to be a US citizen.

** On March 4, 1960, the Belgian ship *La Coubre*, bringing ammunition for the Cuban armed forces, exploded in Havana harbor, killing 72 people and injuring more than 200.

very little petroleum; it has some heavy fuel that can be used to operate its steam-driven machinery and some alcohol that can be used in vehicles; besides, there are large amounts of petroleum in the world. Egypt can sell it, the Soviet Union can sell it, possibly Iraq will be able to sell it soon. It is not possible to develop a purely economic strategy.

Another possible form of aggression to add to this economic variant is an intervention by some puppet power, the Dominican Republic, for example, which would be something of a nuisance; but the United Nations would undoubtedly step in, with nothing concrete having been achieved.·

Incidentally, the new course followed by the Organization of American States creates a dangerous precedent for intervention. Under the cover of the Trujillo pretext, monopoly consoles itself by constructing a means of aggression. It is sad that Venezuelan democracy has put us in the difficult position of having to oppose an intervention against Trujillo. What a good turn it has done the pirates of the continent!

Among the new possibilities for aggression is the assassination of the same old "crazy kid," Fidel Castro, who has now become the focus of the monopolies' fury. Naturally, matters must be arranged so that the other two dangerous "international agents," Raúl Castro and the author, are also eliminated. This solution is appealing; if simultaneous assaults on all three or at least on the principal leader succeeded, it would be a bonus for the reactionaries. (But never forget the people, Messrs. Monopolists and agents, the omnipotent people who in their fury at such a crime would crush and erase all those who had anything to do directly or indirectly with an assault on any of the leaders of the revolution; it would be impossible to restrain them.)

Another feature of the Guatemalan variant is to pressure

the arms suppliers so as to force Cuba to buy from communist countries, and to then use this as an occasion to let loose another torrent of insults. This could produce results. Someone in our government has said, "It might be that they will attack us as communists, but they are not going to eliminate us as imbeciles."

Therefore a direct aggression by the monopolies begins to seem necessary; all the variants are being shuffled and studied in the IBM machines, calculating every result. It occurs to us right now that the Spanish variant could be used. The Spanish variant would be one in which some initial pretext is seized on for an attack by exiles with the help of volunteers, volunteers who would be mercenaries, of course, or simply the troops of a foreign power, well supported by sea and air — we should say, with enough support to be successful. It could also begin as a direct aggression by some state like the Dominican Republic, which would send some men, our brothers, and many mercenaries to die on these beaches in order to provoke a war; this would prompt the "pure-intentioned" monopolists to say that they did not want to intervene in this "disastrous" struggle between brothers; they would merely restrict the war by maintaining vigilance over the skies and seas of this part of America with cruisers, battleships, destroyers, aircraft carriers, submarines, minesweepers, torpedo boats, and airplanes. And it might happen that while these zealous guardians of continental peace were not allowing a single boat to pass carrying anything for Cuba, some, many, or all of the boats headed for the unhappy country of Trujillo would escape the iron vigilance. Also they might intervene through some "reputable" inter-American body, to put an end to the "crazy war" that "communism" had unleashed in our island; or, if this device of the "reputable" American organization was no use, they might intervene directly, as they did in Korea, using the name of the international body in order to restore peace and protect the interests of their citizens.

Perhaps the first step in the aggression will not be against us, but against the constitutional government of Venezuela, in order to remove our last point of support on the continent. If this happens, it is possible that the center of the struggle against colonialism will move from Cuba to the great country of [Simón] Bolívar. The people of Venezuela will rise to defend their liberties with all the enthusiasm of those who know they are fighting a decisive battle, that behind defeat lies the darkest tyranny and behind victory the certain future of America. A wave of popular struggles might disturb the peace of the monopolist cemeteries that our subjugated sister republics have become.

Many factors operate against the enemy's chance of victory, but there are two key ones. First, the external: this is 1960, the year of the underdeveloped peoples, the year of the free people, the year in which there will finally be respect for the voices of the millions of beings who are lucky enough not to be governed by the possessors of the means of death and payment. Furthermore — and this is an even more powerful argument — an army of six million Cubans will grab hold of weapons as a single person in order to defend their territory and their revolution. Cuba will be a battlefield where the army will be nothing other than part of the people in arms; if destroyed in a frontal war, hundreds of guerrilla bands under a dynamic command and a single center of orientation would fight the battle all over the country. In cities the workers will die in their factories or workplaces, and in the countryside the peasants will deal out death to the invader from behind every palm tree and from every furrow of the new mechanically plowed field that the revolution has given them.

And around the world international solidarity will create a barricade of hundreds of millions of people protesting against the aggression. Monopoly will see how its pillars are shaken and how the web of its newspaper lies is blown away by a single puff. But suppose they dare to defy the popular outrage of the world, what will happen then?

The first thing to recognize, considering our position as a very vulnerable island without heavy weapons, with a very weak air force and navy, is the need to apply the concept of guerrilla warfare to the fight for national defense.

Our ground units will fight with all the fervor, commitment, and enthusiasm of which the sons of the Cuban revolution are capable in these glorious years of our history; but in the worst case, we are prepared to continue fighting even after the destruction of our army organization in a frontal combat. In other words, in confronting large concentrations of enemy forces that have succeeded in destroying our army, we would immediately transform ourselves into a guerrilla army with broad mobility, with our column commanders having unlimited authority, although a central command situated somewhere in the country would provide the necessary orders and establish the overall strategy.

The mountains would be the last line of defense of the organized armed vanguard of the people, which is the Rebel Army; but in every house of the people, on every road, in every forest, in every part of our national territory the struggle would be fought by the great army of the rearguard, the entire people trained and armed in the manner now to be described.

As our infantry units will not have heavy arms, they will

concentrate on anti-tank and anti-aircraft defense. Mines in very large numbers, bazookas or anti-tank grenades, highly mobile anti-aircraft cannons and mortar batteries will be our only significant powerful weapons. The veteran infantry soldier, although equipped with automatic weapons, will know the value of ammunition and will guard it with loving care. Special installations for reloading shells will accompany each army unit, maintaining reserves of ammunition, even in these precarious conditions.[7]

The air force will probably be badly hit in the first moments of an invasion of this type. We are basing our calculations upon an invasion by a great foreign power or by a mercenary army of some small power, helped either openly or covertly by this great power. The national air force, as I said, will be destroyed, or almost destroyed; only reconnaissance or liaison planes will remain, especially helicopters for minor functions.

The navy will also be organized for this mobile strategy; small launches will offer the enemy the most minimal target and maintain maximum mobility. In such circumstances, the enemy army becomes desperate to find something to receive its blows; all he will find is a mobile, impenetrable, gelatinous mass that retreats and never presents a solid front, while inflicting wounds from every side.

It is not easy to overpower an army of the people that is prepared to continue as an army in spite of defeat in a frontal battle. Two great masses of the people are united around it: the peasants and the workers. The peasants have already shown their effectiveness in capturing the small band that was marauding in Pinar del Rio. These peasants will be trained

---

7. This paragraph is marked with a green line with the observation: **Comment.**

principally in their own regions; but the platoon commanders and the superior officers will be trained, as is now already being done, in our military bases. From there they will be distributed throughout the 30 zones of agrarian development that form the new geographical division of the country. These will constitute 30 more centers of peasant struggle, charged with defending to the last their lands, their social conquests, their new houses, their canals, their dams, their ripening harvests, their independence, in a word, their right to live.

At the beginning they will present a firm resistance to any enemy advance, but if this proves too strong for them, they will disperse, each peasant becoming a peaceful cultivator of the soil during the day and a fearsome guerrilla fighter at night, the scourge of the enemy forces. Something similar will take place among the workers; the best among them will also be trained to act as leaders of their compañeros, teaching them the principles of defense. Each social class, however, will have different tasks. The peasant will fight the typical battle of the guerrilla fighter; he should learn to be a good shot, to take advantage of all the difficulties of the terrain and to disappear without ever showing his face. The workers, on the other hand, have the advantage of operating in a modern city, a large and efficient fortress; at the same time their lack of mobility is a handicap. The worker will learn first to blockade the streets with barricades of any available vehicle, furniture, or utensil; to use every block as a fortress with communications through holes made in interior walls; to use that terrible defense weapon, the "Molotov cocktail"; and to coordinate gunfire from the innumerable crevices provided by the houses of a modern city.

From the worker masses assisted by the national police and those armed forces charged with the defense of the city, a powerful block of the army will be created; but it should expect to suffer great losses. The struggle in the cities in these conditions cannot achieve the facility and flexibility of the struggle in the countryside: many will fall, including many leaders, in this popular struggle. The enemy will use tanks that will be destroyed rapidly as soon as the people learn their weaknesses and not to fear them; but before that the tanks will leave their tally of victims.

There will be other organizations linked to those of the workers and peasants: first, the student militias, which will contain the flower of the student youth, directed and coordinated by the Rebel Army; organizations of youth in general, who will participate in the same way; and organizations of women, who will provide great encouragement by their presence and who will do such auxiliary tasks for their compañeros in the struggle as cooking, taking care of the wounded, giving final comfort to those who are dying, doing laundry, in a word, showing their compañeros-in-arms that they will never be absent in the difficult times of the revolution. All this is achieved by the widespread organization of the masses supplemented by patient and careful education, an education that begins and is confirmed in knowledge acquired from their own experience; it must focus on rational and truthful explanations of the facts of the revolution.

The revolutionary laws should be discussed, explained, studied in every meeting, in every assembly, wherever the leaders of the revolution are present for any purpose. Further-more, the speeches of the leaders, and in our case particularly of the undisputed leader, should constantly be read, commented on, and discussed. People should gather together in the country-side to listen to the radio, and where there is more advanced technology, to watch on television those magnificent popular lessons given by our prime minister [Fidel Castro].

The participation of the people in politics, that is to say, in the expression of their own desires made into laws, decrees, and resolutions, must be constant. Vigilance against any manifestation of opposition to the revolution should also be constant; and vigilance over morale within the revolutionary masses should be stricter, if this is possible, than vigilance against the non-revolutionary or the disaffected. If the revolution is not to take the dangerous path of opportunism, it can never be allowed that a revolutionary of any level should be excused for grave offenses of conduct or morality simply because they are a revolutionary. Their former service record might provide extenuating circumstances and can always be taken into consideration in deciding on the punishment, but the act itself must always be punished.

Respect for work, especially for collective work and work for collective ends, should be cultivated. Volunteer brigades to construct roads, bridges, docks or dams, and school cities should receive a strong impulse; this helps to forge unity among those people who demonstrate their love for the revolution by their works.

An army connected in this way to the people, that feels an intimacy with the peasants and the workers from which it has arisen, that knows all the special techniques of warfare and is psychologically prepared for the worst contingencies, knows itself to be invincible. And it will become even more invincible as the army and the citizenry embody the righteous phrase of our immortal Camilo: "The army is the people in uniform." For this, for all this, in spite of the monopolists' desire to suppress Cuba's "bad example," our future shines brighter than ever.

Also by Ernesto 'Che' Guevara

The Motorcycle Diaries

In January 1952, two young men from Buenos Aires set out to explore South America on 'La Poderosa', the Powerful One: a 500cc Norton. One of them was the 23-year-old Che Guevara.

Written eight years before the Cuban Revolution, these are Che's diaries – full of disasters and discoveries, high drama, low comedy and laddish improvisations. During his travels through Argentina, Chile, Peru and Venezuela, Che's main concerns are where the next drink is coming from, where the next bed is to be found and who might be around to share it.

Within a decade the whole world would know his name. His trip might have been an adventure of a lifetime – had his lifetime not turned into a much greater adventure ...

'*Easy Rider* meets *Das Kapital*'   *The Times*

'A revolutionary bestseller'   *Guardian*

Reminiscences of the Cuban Revolutionary War

The Authorised Edition

This is Che Guevara's gripping account of the Cuban Revolution – from the inside out. Between 1956 and 1959, and against immense odds, he and his band of guerrillas fought with the people of Cuba to emerge victorious from years of brutal dictatorship, poverty, and corruption.

Che recounts their careful planning and bloody battles, fought in all kinds of weather, on all kinds of terrain. They dealt with sickness and deserters, recruiting peasants and punishing traitors. And as the story unfolds, we witness Che's transformation from troop doctor to iconic revolutionary.

'Che's life is an inspiration for every human being who loves freedom. We will always honour his memory'   NELSON MANDELA

'Powerful and poetic … For anyone interested in the myth of Che Guevara, and in the idea that a small group of determined men can take over a country, this book is essential reading'
COLM TOIBIN, *Observer*

The Bolivian Diary

The Authorised Edition

With an Introduction by Fidel Castro

This is Che Guevara's famous last diary, found in his backpack when he was captured, arrested and subsequently executed by the Bolivian army in October 1967. Published after his death, it catapulted Che to iconic status throughout the world.

In November 1966, Che arrived in Bolivia to lead a guerrilla force, fighting that country's military dictatorship. At first, they won their battles, outwitting the vastly superior forces surrounding them. Gradually, however, the army began to surround them, and their situation became more and more desperate.

Here, in Che's own words, are the events leading up to those final days. Told with honesty and humility, it is a remarkable record of heroism and bravery.

'Guevara was a figure of epic proportions. These diaries, stark and moving, will be his most enduring monument'   *Observer*

'Vivid and compelling'   *Economist*